SALTWATER
LEADERSHIP

TITLES IN THE SERIES

THE U.S. NAVAL INSTITUTE BLUE & GOLD
PROFESSIONAL LIBRARY

FOR MORE THAN 100 YEARS, U.S. NAVY PROFESSIONALS have counted on specialized books published by the Naval Institute Press to prepare them for their responsibilities as they advance in their careers and to serve as ready references and refreshers when needed. From the days of coal-fired battleships to the era of unmanned aerial vehicles and laser weaponry, such perennials as *The Bluejacket's Manual* and the *Watch Officer's Guide* have guided generations of Sailors through the complex challenges of naval service. As these books are updated and new ones are added to the list, they will carry the distinctive mark of the Blue and Gold Professional Library series to remind and reassure their users that they have been prepared by naval professionals and meet the exacting standards that Sailors have long expected from the U.S. Naval Institute.

SALTWATER LEADERSHIP

A PRIMER ON LEADERSHIP FOR THE JUNIOR SEA-SERVICE OFFICER

RADM Robert O. Wray Jr., USN

Naval Institute Press
Annapolis, Maryland

Naval Institute Press
291 Wood Road
Annapolis, MD 21402

Library of Congress Cataloging-in-Publication Data
Wray, Robert O., Jr.
  Saltwater leadership : a primer on leadership for the young sea-service officer / written and edited by Robert O. Wray Jr.
    pages cm
  Includes bibliographical references and index.
  ISBN 978-1-61251-212-9 (hbk. : alk. paper) — ISBN 978-1-61251-213-6 (ebook) 1. United States. Navy—Officers' handbooks 2. Merchant marine—United States—Officers—Handbooks, manuals, etc. 3. Leadership—Handbooks, manuals, etc. 4. United States. Navy—Sea life—Anecdotes. 5. Naval art and science—Handbooks, manuals, etc. I. Title.
  V133.W73 2012
  359.3'3041—dc23
                                    2013001681

26 25 24 23 22 21 20 19   12 11 10 9 8 7 6 5

This book is dedicated to all those who go to sea
in ships and to those who lead them.

In particular to my son Jack, on a Navy frigate in the Pacific
and to my nephew Zach, at Maine Maritime Academy
on his way toward a Coast Guard cutter.

One hundred percent of the royalties from this book
will be donated to charities that support Sailors and mariners,
including the Navy and Marine Corps Relief Society,
the Coast Guard Foundation, and the United Seaman's Service.

CONTENTS

FOREWORD

From the maxims of Publilius Syrus to the insights of Dale Carnegie, the rhumb lines of Arleigh Burke to the contemporary advice of James Stavridis, *Saltwater Leadership* contains lessons from the most revered thought-leaders and valued sources and condenses them into chapters that you can absorb and understand between watches or sorties. *Saltwater Leadership* will provide you with the insights of hundreds of senior sea service leaders and the instruments to chart a course toward your own leadership horizon.

A lesson in leadership that has influenced me throughout my life came from my grandfather, Admiral John S. McCain Sr., who commanded a carrier task force in the Pacific during World War II. After pilots returned from strikes he would seek them out, asking them, 'Do you think we're doing the right thing?' He knew that if he ever stopped learning from his men, then he stopped leading.

Whether exercised in self-discipline or over the forces of a combatant command, leadership is vital, and the challenges and opportunities of the future demand it. I hope you take these lessons to heart—in my experience, the wisdom in these pages can give you strength and hope during the most challenging of times.

John McCain
United States Senator

PREFACE

Three caveats to the material enclosed herein:

The word "primer," according to *Webster's*, is "a small introductory book on a subject," from the Medieval Latin *primarium*. This book is intended as a primer. In no way does it deserve to sit alongside such great leadership texts as Montor's *Naval Leadership*, which took dozens of people dozens of years to produce. It is intended as a short, simple book that can be read in five-minute snippets by a busy young officer at sea.

Much of the material in this book is Navy-centric. This has three causes: First, I have served in the Navy for more than thirty years, and many of the contributors to this book responded because they knew me from prior service together. Second, due to its size the Navy has more officers serving at sea today than either the Coast Guard or the U.S. Merchant Marine, and therefore a preponderance of officers-at-sea stories come from that greater population. And third, the Navy has been more prolific in the generation of books about leadership than either the Coast Guard or the Merchant Marine service; because this book provides an overview of some of the existing literature, it therefore becomes more Navy-oriented. In any case, this is a book for junior officers at sea, regardless of service type or agency. I have tried to make the stories and lessons applicable to all, regardless of their source. I believe that any young graduate from Kings Point can learn a lesson from a Coast Guard cutter in the Caribbean, just as a graduate from an NROTC unit can learn seagoing lessons from deep-draft tankers in Alaskan waters.

In a similar way, much of the material and many of the stories and quotations reflect the previous all-male character of the seagoing service. Quotes from the eighteenth and nineteenth centuries didn't anticipate women at sea, and even today's senior officers served as junior officers on ships without women. Across all the services, the number of women serving as officers on ships is increasing rapidly; indeed, at a recent ship-selection event by Naval Academy midshipmen, fifty-eight of the top one hundred graduates (and hence the first pickers of ships) were women! I have tried to make this book useful to all officers, regardless of gender, and ask your forbearance in appreciating the good ideas from literature whose language is now out of date.

SALTWATER
LEADERSHIP

INTRODUCTION

This book is about leadership, written for young officers at sea. It is not intended to be an academic text. As you will see, it is certainly not a work of literature. It is intended to be functional, simple, down to earth, and easy to digest. Straightforward, basic truths, without frills.

Leadership deals with the very nature of humanity, with what we are here for, with how we should interact with other humans, with what we should do in this world. It is serious, and some books on leadership necessarily deal with the philosophic and existential issues of why humans do what they do, and how. Leadership strikes at the heart of humanity and vice versa. It can be a satisfying and worthwhile study.

Other books focus on the more pedestrian, more pragmatic view of leadership: What is it? How can we describe it? How can we identify the successful ways of leadership? And, more important, how can we become successful leaders?

This book focuses on the latter view, specifically for young officers at sea. I have been where you are—I know your busy life might not leave room for reading the classic texts to learn leadership. Instead, this book attempts to offer you some simple leadership lessons, in bite-sized chunks that can be taken and digested between watches and sea evolutions and during the few minutes each day that you might have to yourself. Perhaps those small chunks will whet your appetite.

Given that limited aim, I hope this book meets the mark for you.

CHAPTER 1

LEADERSHIP FOR
YOUNG OFFICERS AT SEA

A leader is best
When people barely know that he exists,
Not so good when people obey and acclaim him,
Worst when they despise him.

"Fail to honor people,
They fail to honor you";

But of a good leader, who talks little,
When his work is done, his aim fulfilled,
They will all say, "We did this ourselves."

—LAO TZU, *TAO TEH CHING*,
VERSE 17, 6TH CENTURY BC

This chapter does four things to get you started. It

– gives you the bottom line up front on leadership,

– answers the six basic questions on leadership,

– describes some basic models we can use to describe leadership, and

– explains how this book is organized and where we'll go from here.

So let's get started!

THE BOTTOM LINE, UP FRONT

This is the bottom line, right here on the first page:

Leadership matters. Everything in the world happens because of leadership.

Leadership is definable. It's not some hocus-pocus touchy-feely amorphous state of mind or relationship. It can be described and defined. It can be measured.

You can be a leader. It's learnable. You don't have to be born with it. Whatever you are today, you can become a leader, if you choose.

You, too, can make things happen.

Winston Churchill said, in writing to young officers like you: "Come on now all you young people all over the world. You have not an hour to lose. You must take your place in Life's fighting line. Twenty to twenty five! Those are the years. Don't be content with things as they are. Don't take No for an answer. Never submit to failure. You will make all kinds of mistakes; but as long as you are generous and true and also fierce, you cannot hurt the world!"

Are you ready to make things happen? Are you ready to be generous and true and fierce?

Are you ready to be a leader at sea?

You can be. Read this book!

THE SIX BASIC QUESTIONS

"What is leadership, anyway?"

A good question. One that many people have studied for many years. There are a hundred definitions.

Webster's defines leadership as "the act of being a leader" and defines a leader as a person "with commanding authority or influence."

According to Navy General Order 21 (as first issued), leadership is defined as "the art of accomplishing the Navy's mission through people."

In the Commandant Instruction on leadership, the Coast Guard says leadership is "the ability to influence others to obtain their obedience, respect, confidence, and loyal cooperation."

The Army says that leadership is "influencing people—by providing purpose, direction, and motivation—while operating to accomplish the mission and improving the organization."

In my midshipman leadership text written several decades ago, leadership was somewhat loftily defined as "the art, science, or gift by which a person is enabled and privileged to direct the thoughts, plans, and actions of others in such a manner as to obtain and command their obedience, their confidence, their respect, and their loyal cooperation."

Leading sailors is an art, not a science.

—*RADM Arleigh Burke*

Field Marshal Bernard Montgomery said, "Leadership is the capacity and will to rally men and women to a common purpose and the character which inspires confidence." Similarly, Dwight Eisenhower said, "Leadership is the art of getting someone else to do something you want done because he wants to do it." Finally, Harry Truman echoed Eisenhower almost word for word when he said, "A leader is a man who has the ability to get other people to do what they don't want to do, and like it."

In other words: Leadership is the *process* of getting *people* to *do* things.

Now that might seem manipulative, crass, simplistic. Maybe it is. But in the end, things happen only because people make them happen, and someone has to get those people to make them happen. That's where leadership comes in.

"What's the difference between leadership and management?"

Another good question, and one often asked by junior officers. Like anything having to do with leadership, there are plenty of different answers. Some say that leadership is deciding *what* to do, and *why*, while management focuses on *how*.

Some say leadership focuses on accomplishing the mission, while management is about doing it efficiently.

Management author Ken Adelman says, "A leader knows what's best to do; a manager knows how best to do it."

Some say that leadership is about influencing, while management is more about operating. But notice that the Army definition of leadership cited previously includes both influencing and operating.

Renowned Harvard professor and leadership expert John Kotter says that management is about running things in steady state, while leadership is about causing change.

Management guru Warren Bennis laid out the following distinctions between the two:

- Leaders do the right things; managers do things right.

- Leaders innovate; managers administer.

- Leaders inspire; managers control.

- Leaders think long-term; managers think short-term.

- Leaders originate; managers imitate.

- Leaders challenge the status quo; managers accept the status quo.

A manager's job is to create stability and deal with reality.
A leader's job is to stir emotion and set audacious, grandiose
goals that shake the status quo. Too much management
and you stagnate. Too much leadership and you get nowhere.
Embrace the challenge of striking the balance. Do it well,
and the results will surpass your wildest dreams.

—*The Management and Leadership Network*

As usual, all these views are right, in their own way. For the junior officer, you will be providing both management and leadership to the folks who work for you, and often the two will overlap. For instance, say you're working on a tough project and one of your key people has a family situation that needs attention. Deciding to let him go tend to his family, even if it hurts your team strength, is a leadership decision. Figuring out how to adjust other team schedules to make it work is more about management.

"Why is leadership important?"

In the world of the junior officer at sea, does leadership really matter? Isn't it really about standing a good watch and managing the few people that might work for you?

Leadership is important to you in two ways.

First, it will help you do your job better, today. You are not in charge of three bookkeepers in office cubicles, working nine-to-five weekdays. Management alone could probably get that job done.

Rather, you are responsible for far more people, under far more arduous, difficult, and unpredictable circumstances. You and your ship are working 24/7, year-round, in bad weather, in difficult situations, in conflict, sometimes under adversity, or even under fire. These conditions call for more than management. Your decisions can place your people into danger. Sending a mariner topside at night in freezing foul weather to find and fix a thorny problem isn't management—it takes leadership to have influence like that. Leading a team into a smoke-filled space to put out a fire isn't management; it's leadership, pure and simple.

Being a leader is critical to get your job done, even as the most junior officer on your ship. If you need further evidence, look at your performance evaluation. Is there a block for "management"? Probably not. Is there a block to evaluate you in leadership? Absolutely.

Second, leadership is important to you today because in most cases, it is the coin of the realm for your advancement in the sea services. The path to the top is built of critical leadership steps, without which you'll never progress. Whether your goal is to become a master or chief engineer of a ship, or a captain in the Coast Guard or Navy, you can't do it without successfully demonstrating leadership at every level as you progress.

I consider it a great advantage to obtain command young, having observed as a general thing that persons who come into authority late in life shrink from responsibility, and often break down under its weight.

—*ADM David Farragut*

"Is leadership innate or learned?"

It's 3 percent innate and 97 percent learned.

Those numbers aren't exact, obviously—they're my view, and as you'll find in leadership study, everyone has a different point of view. But based on my forty years of leadership experience and study, they're pretty close.

Some inherited traits are helpful. For instance, it helps if you're tall. The overwhelming majority of presidential elections have been won by the taller candidate. In the corporate marketplace, taller people, overall, get paid slightly more, and are promoted slightly more often. Statistically, physical attractiveness is similarly rewarded.

It also helps if you're intelligent. Intelligence can help you to be a better communicator, a better solver of problems. It helps you to learn leadership skills faster. There is a positive correlation between intelligence and advancement in corporate management hierarchies. In other words, senior managers, in general, score higher in intelligence tests than middle managers. Similarly, chief executives are, in general, measurably smarter than senior managers.

Finally, for some circumstances, it helps if you're big and strong. In some groups, size and strength can assist in leadership. In other groups, it's immaterial.

But that's about it. All the other leadership traits—character, speaking ability, empathy, organization, vision, honesty, work ethic, amiability, courage, perseverance—are all acquired. They are all learned. They are all available to you. If you didn't get them growing up, you can get them now, if you choose.

"How does one become a leader?"

If you wanted to play the piano, what would you do? Most likely, you would:

- study a book on music and theory
- get a teacher to give you lessons
- practice the piano
- watch and listen to others play

If you want to learn French, if you want to become a chef, if you want to hit a curveball, if you want to learn virtually anything, it might include:

- study
- a teacher
- practice
- observation of others

So it is with leadership. Leadership can be learned using these four basic tenets.

COL Art Athens, a leadership professor at the Naval Academy and former commandant of the Merchant Marine Academy at Kings Point, has written in his book *Preparing to Lead* that leadership can be learned through six fundamental building blocks:

1. self-knowledge
2. observation
3. intellectual base
4. mentoring
5. adversity
6. experience

His six building blocks are nouns—they are results that provide the foundation of leadership. My four items above—studying, getting taught, practicing, and observing—are verbs. They are what you, the young officer at sea, can *do* to acquire those six building blocks.

Remember, you can become a leader. You can learn. You do it by:

- studying leadership
- having a mentor or a teacher who can help you perfect your skills
- practicing and experiencing leadership
- watching other leaders around you, both good and bad

SPOM: Study, Practice, Observe, Mentor. It's not rocket science. But, by the way, if you wanted to learn rocket science, you'd learn it the same way!

One note: the four steps above all require one thing: *will*. You have to *want* to be a leader. You don't become one through osmosis or through mere wishful thinking. You can wish you were a great piano player, but unless you take the steps to make it happen, it won't happen. ADM William Pratt, former chief of Naval Operations, said, "Few realize that the growth to sound leadership is a life's work. Ambition alone will not encompass it. [It] is a long, hard road to travel."

Leadership and learning are indispensable to each other.

—*John F. Kennedy*

"Why another book on leadership?"

A very good question. One could argue that the world doesn't need another book on leadership. There are business leadership books and academic leadership books and theoretical leadership books and military leadership books. Why another?

This is the only leadership book written specifically for you young officers at sea, on ships, in the Navy, the Coast Guard, and the U.S. Merchant Marine. Your conditions are different; your needs are different. Leadership lessons and concepts can be universal, but this book is written specifically for you, in two ways.

First, the lessons and concepts are placed in the shipboard context in which you lead your lives. You could potentially learn leadership lessons by reading about business leaders or about Air Force officers flying jets, but you'll learn those lessons better if you hear from people who have worn your shoes and lived your life.

Second, the book is written in a format with your life in mind. You're busy and tired and not all that interested in reading a nine-hundred-page footnoted tome about leadership. In your life today, short and sweet and to the point is better.

> No man is a leader until his appointment is ratified in the minds and hearts of his men.
>
> —Infantry Journal, *1948*

So, another leadership book, but one that will hopefully fit your life and needs. And, when your needs go beyond the simplicities of this primer, you'll be able to use the leadership lists from chapters 2 and 6 for more information.

SOME WAYS OF LOOKING AT LEADERSHIP

We saw before that there are a number of definitions for leadership. There are also a number of different ways to talk about it. They're called "models," or paradigms, or conceptual frameworks. They are a way to make the complex more understandable. Choose which one works for you, or create your own.

Model 1: It's about Who You Are

This model is the "great man" model of leadership. Ancient storytellers, and early modern leadership studies, felt that leadership consisted of a great human who was blessed with a list of attributes such as character, honesty, bravery, oratory, kindness, strength, and other noble characteristics. Discussions tended to center on whether the great human was born with those traits, or whether he or she acquired them. In this model, your leadership is all about who you are.

Model 2: It's about Traits and Skills and Circumstances

This more nuanced model says that being a leader is about certain innate traits (such as honesty), certain skills that can be learned (like public speaking), and how the leader uses those skills according to the individual circumstance (as in a crisis, or a death, or corporate transition). It's not all traits, and yet not all skills. And, regardless of traits and skills, the circumstances count; what works in battle might not work in the boardroom and vice versa.

Leadership is a process of persuasion and example, by which others are motivated to take action.

—*John Gardner, Ron Heifetz*

Model 3: It's about the Leader, the Follower, the Situation

This model emphasizes the relationship between the leader and his or her followers, and the situation in which they are all placed. The traits and skills of the leader aren't absolute, according to this model. They work only when they are matched with the followers: the traits and skills that work with shipboard engineers are not the ones that succeed in coaching a women's high school basketball team. In this paradigm, leaders succeed only when they are placed in front of the right group of followers, and placed in a situation in which both fit and can excel.

Model 4: It's Be–Know–Do!

This model is the Army model described in its field manual on leadership. And, like some other models, it emphasizes both who you are, what you know, and the actions you take. "Be" is the human that you are, the traits you possess. "Know" is the leadership skills you've developed through study and practice, such as delegation and recognition. "Do" is the action you take to fit the situation in which you and your followers are placed. The question then becomes: What should you be? What should you know? What should you do? Those answers are provided in the field manual.

LEADERSHIP IS PRONE TO LISTS

One thing is certain: a discussion of leadership is prone to produce lists.

What's the perfect house? Well, it depends. What is perfect for one person might be anathema for another. However, if we're unable to "define" a perfect home, we can at least provide a list of home characteristics that most people find perfect in most situations, such as a fireplace, a modern kitchen, multiple bedrooms, large rooms, a big-screen TV, walk-in closets, a two-car garage, windows with a view, energy efficiency, and so on. Faced with something too difficult to describe exactly and universally, we search for a list of attributes.

So it is with leadership. We can't define it exactly, because it means so many things to so many people under so many circumstances. But we can list attributes that great leaders seem to share. We can list skills that leaders seem to employ. We can list actions that leaders often take. We can list circumstances in which leadership has an effect. We can list triggers and sets of rules that seem to connect skill and action and effect.

Characteristics of a Boy Scout:			
Trustworthy	Friendly	Obedient	Brave
Loyal	Courteous	Cheerful	Clean
Helpful	Kind	Thrifty	Reverent

—Boy Scout Handbook

The great pointillist painters didn't paint in brush-strokes—they created tiny dots of paint that cumulatively created an expansive and perfectly understandable picture. Close up, all one sees is dots; from a distance, the image becomes clear. Defining leadership by lists seems to accomplish the same thing.

In reviewing books on leadership I was struck by the lists. In trying to get senior seagoing officers to define leadership for you, the junior officer, I was forced into yet another list—a list of potential attributes. Additional chapters provide a list of sea stories, a list of pieces of advice from senior officers, and finally, a list of advice from me on how you might become the leader you want to be.

Leadership: it's hard to define. So embrace the lists, and the utility thereof!

HOW THIS BOOK IS STRUCTURED

This book is organized into two watches, ten simple and relatively stand-alone chapters.

Chapter 1, as you have read, attempts to answer the six basic questions about leadership and to provide an overview of the basic study and modeling of leadership. It is the barest-of-basic summary of leadership, just to establish a simple foundation.

> An army formed with good officers moves like clockwork.
>
> —*GEN George Washington*

After that summary, there are two basic watches—starboard and port—and each contains four chapters.

1. Each watch includes a chapter with a list of leadership lists. These cumulative lists include traits, skills, circumstances, and rules. They attempt to summarize lessons from about thirty-five leadership books, comprising some ten thousand pages of information.

2. Each watch contains a chapter of sea stories from seagoing officers. Each story illustrates a leadership trait or attribute or skill or practice. A story about "praising in public" and the penalty for failing to observe that rule will perhaps be more effective for you than simply another textbook admonition to do the same.

3. Each watch contains a chapter listing brief pieces of salty advice from the same group of senior seagoing officers. These one-page memos of advice answer the question "If you had only one page of advice to give to a young new officer at sea, what would you say?"

4. Finally, each watch contains a chapter "What Seniors Say." In the Starboard watch, chapter 5 includes the newest leadership list, representing about nine thousand years of experience of seagoing officers. It tries to answer the question "What traits and attributes are most important to a young officer at sea?" It provides a survey of 380 officers, each of which cast sixteen votes against seventy different attributes. It provides the results of their cumulative wisdom. In the Port watch, chapter 9 provides another set of leadership advice from great minds through the ages, including Theodore Roosevelt, Winston Churchill, George

Washington, Andrew Carnegie, George Patton, and others.

Chapter 10 will conclude with a potential game plan for you. A plan to help you become all the leader that you can be—all the leader that your country, and your shipmates, need you to be.

THE FIRST WATCH

STARBOARD

0800–1200

CHAPTER 2

THE LEADERSHIP LISTS

Officers and others in authority in the naval service are required to show in themselves a good example of virtue, honor, patriotism, and subordination.

They will be vigilant in inspecting the conduct of all persons; they will guard against and suppress dissolute and immoral practices according to regulations.

They will take all necessary and proper measures under the laws, regulations, and customs to promote and safeguard the moral, physical well-being, and general welfare of the officers and enlisted personnel under their command.

—TITLE 10, *U.S. CODE*

At the end of the previous chapter we noted that leadership can be an ethereal concept which, oddly enough, lends itself to lists.

Also, please remember that the premise to this primer on leadership is that you are too busy to spend hundreds of hours reading books on leadership. Your life is out there, away from study, standing watch, leading your troops, tending to the ship, and maybe catching some liberty (or some sleep) now and then.

With those two thoughts in mind, the next few pages condense 35 books about leadership into several buckets of condensed thought. More precisely, they present the "lists" of leadership traits, attributes, practices, rules, and concepts provided in these books. These 35 books don't represent the totality of all thought on leadership (as of this writing, there were 60,000 leadership books listed on Amazon.com!). However, the 35 books represent a good mix of books that the young officer might find interesting and germane.

Those books come in three basic groups: (1) books from the sea services, (2) books from other services, and (3) business and academic books. A complete list is provided in appendix B. Together, those books include hundreds of different leadership lists, many of which are provided to you in this summary.

Discipline begins in the Wardroom. I dread not the seamen.
It is in the indiscreet conversations of the officers
and their presumptuous discussions of the orders
they receive that produce all our ills.

—*Lord St. Vincent*

The wisdom of the many leadership lists in those books seems to fall into four categories:

1. Qualities and Attributes of leaders—what they seem to be
2. Leadership Competencies—what they do
3. Advice, Principles, Rules, Recommendations— how leaders should behave
4. Models of Leadership

In this chapter, we'll look at the first two categories: Attributes and Competencies. In chapter 6 of the Port watch, we'll look at the second two categories: Advice, Rules, and Models.

No one human is qualified to give you the definitive list of attributes of a leader. It doesn't exist. However, by scanning the lists that accrue from the thirty-five collective works of dozens of authors that represent hundreds of years of effort and wisdom, you can begin to see trends and commonalities that can inform your own definition of what leadership is. These two chapters condense about ten thousand pages of information and summarize them into just a few.

So, read on through the lists, and find the nuggets of truth that ring most true to you.

QUALITIES AND ATTRIBUTES

As we've mentioned before, it's hard to say exactly what leadership is, but all authors on leadership seem to have their own list of the qualities, or the attributes, of a leader. In fact, eight of the thirty-five books had a definitive "qualities of a leader" list.

Was there commonality or consensus among those eight lists? You bet.

Of the eight lists, six included the following attributes as necessary qualities:

- Integrity and Character
- Endurance, Tenacity, Stamina, Stick-to-it-iveness

I divide officers into four classes—the clever, the lazy, the stupid, and the industrious. Each officer possesses at least two of these qualities.

—*Kurt von Hammerstein-Equord*

Five of the eight lists agreed on the following attributes:

- Physical Courage
- Initiative
- Knowledge and Intelligence
- Maturity and Judgment
- Self-Discipline

Finally, four of the eight lists included the following common traits:

- Moral Courage
- Decisiveness
- Loyalty
- Enthusiasm and Optimism
- Selflessness
- Ability to Communicate, both in speaking and writing

This baker's dozen of attributes, listed above, was common throughout the lists in these leadership books and appeared time and time again throughout all the other books. If you're looking for a list of attributes you want to cultivate, consider the thirteen above!

That's the summary. Now let's glance over some specifics. First, let's look at what books on Navy leadership have to say.

The Naval Officer's Guide, edited by CDR Lesa McComas, covers all the nuances of being a naval officer. Chapter 18 covers leadership and lists the following nineteen attributes or traits of the successful seagoing leader:

1. Knowledge
2. Integrity
3. Loyalty
4. Maturity
5. Will
6. Followership
7. Self-Discipline
8. Confidence
9. Flexibility
10. Endurance
11. Decisiveness

12. Initiative
13. Justice
14. Compassion
15. Forcefulness
16. Positive Attitude
17. Communication Skills
18. Personal Behavior (ethical and moral)
19. Courage (physical and moral)

A good plan violently executed now is better than
a perfect plan next week.

—*GEN George S. Patton*

⚓

The textbook *Fundamentals of Naval Leadership,* edited by the legendary Naval Academy leadership professor Karel Montor, has a similar list:

1. Integrity
2. Dependability
3. Cooperation
4. Loyalty
5. Unselfishness
6. Sense of Humor
7. Tact
8. Ability to Write well
9. Ability to Speak effectively
10. Initiative
11. Judgment
12. Enthusiasm
13. Creativity
14. Decisiveness
15. Endurance
16. Self-Discipline

17. Moral Courage

18. Physical Courage

———————⚓———————

Professor Montor and a team interviewed dozens of senior naval officers to produce the textbook *Naval Leadership: Voices of Experience.* In it, there were four different lists of attributes worth noting:

The Basis of Leadership	Other Requirements for Effective Leadership
Personal Example	Physical Stamina
Moral Responsibility	Mental Stamina
Good Management	Putting Others before Self
Tact	Working Harder than Subordinates
Dependability	Objectivity
Sense of Humor	Accountability
Components of Professionalism	**Characteristics of a Naval Officer**
Integrity	Judgment
Pride	Imagination
Expertise	Analytical Ability
Loyalty to Country	Impeccable Personal Behavior
Pleasure in Work	Military Bearing
Self-Improvement	Forcefulness
Selecting and Utilizing Staff	Speaking and Writing Ability
Members	Self-Improvement
Self-Discipline	Correcting Perceived Wrongs

———————⚓———————

Finally among naval texts, the book *Command at Sea,* written by ADM James Stavridis and RDML Robert Girrier, identifies eight "distinctly American" naval leadership traditions that have applied to American ship captains over the ages:

1. Use of the Initiative
2. Boldness and Daring
3. Tenacity
4. Courage
5. Assertiveness
6. Ingenuity
7. Initiative of Juniors
8. Decision Making

No man is worth his salt who is not ready at all times to risk his well-being, to risk his body, to risk his life, in a great cause.

—*Theodore Roosevelt*

What about traits and attributes identified from other services besides the Navy?

Coast Guard ADM James Loy in the excellent text *Character in Action: The Coast Guard on Leadership* writes that one should look for seven qualities in the people a leader chooses to be around him or her. They are:

1. Intelligence
2. High Energy
3. Self-Confidence
4. Continual Learning
5. Compassion
6. Courage with a Bias Toward Action
7. Character

The *U.S. Army Leadership Field Manual* lists the following attributes of a leader:

1. Will
2. Self-Discipline

3. Initiative
4. Judgment
5. Self-Confidence
6. Cultural Awareness
7. Intelligence
8. Health and Physical Fitness
9. Military and Professional Bearing
10. Self-Control
11. Balance
12. Stability

Another great list from the Army comes from GEN George Patton, in *Patton on Leadership*. The general's personal list of the "chief qualities of leadership" reads as follows:

1. Perfection of detail (being able to pay attention to the little things)
2. Personal supervision
3. Thorough and detailed knowledge of the business at hand
4. A strong physical leadership presence
5. The ability to set a personal example
6. The ability to communicate, to explain orders
7. The commitment to ensure that orders are correctly executed

---

Give every man thine ear, but few thy voice.

—*Shakespeare*

On a more current, less military note, *Leadership for Dummies* has a somewhat different viewpoint in its "Ten Characteristics of a True Leader":

1. Eagerness
2. Cheerfulness
3. Honesty
4. Resourcefulness
5. Persuasiveness
6. Cooperation
7. Altruism
8. Courage
9. Supportiveness
10. Assertiveness

⚓

Notice how we've seen some traits listed before, like honesty, courage, and assertiveness. But others provide a different view—for instance, eagerness? altruism? Once again, leadership looks different to different viewers.

⚓

Rather than rely on an individual's view of what constitutes leadership, the college postgraduate leadership textbook *The Nature of Leadership* identifies a list of approximately twenty key attributes of a leader, as determined by empirical studies over the last twenty years. The twenty attributes fall into six primary buckets:

1. Cognitive Capacities
   - General intelligence
   - Creative thinking
2. Personality
   - Extroversion
   - Conscientiousness
   - Emotional stability
   - Openness
   - Agreeableness

- Tested preferences for extroversion, intuition, thinking, and judging
3. Motives and Needs
   - Need for power
   - Need for achievement
   - Motivation to lead
4. Social Capacities
   - Self-monitoring
   - Social intelligence
   - Emotional intelligence
5. Problem-Solving Skills
   - Problem construction
   - Solution generation
   - Metacognition
6. Tacit Knowledge

Superiority of material strength is given to a commander gratis.
Superior knowledge and superior tactical skill he must
himself acquire. Superior morale, superior cooperation,
he must himself create.

—*ADM Joseph "Bull" Reeves*

One of my favorite leadership lists comes from the well-written and aptly named business book, *The 21 Indispensable Qualities of a Leader* by John C. Maxwell. The list is provided here in its entirety:

1. Character: Be a Piece of the Rock
2. Charisma: The First Impression Can Seal the Deal
3. Commitment: It Separates Doers from Dreamers
4. Communication: Without It You Travel Alone
5. Competence: If You Build It, They Will Come
6. Courage: One Person with Courage Is a Majority
7. Discernment: Put an End to Unsolved Mysteries

8. Focus: The Sharper It Is, the Sharper You Are
9. Generosity: Your Candle Loses Nothing When It Lights Another
10. Initiative: You Won't Leave Home Without It
11. Listening: To Connect with Their Hearts, Use Your Ears
12. Passion: Take This Life and Love It
13. Positive Attitude: If You Believe You Can, You Can
14. Problem Solving: You Can't Let Your Problems Be a Problem
15. Relationships: If You Get Along, They'll Go Along
16. Responsibility: If You Won't Carry the Ball, You Can't Lead the Team
17. Security: Competence Never Compensates for Insecurity
18. Self-Discipline: The First Person You Lead Is You
19. Servanthood: To Get Ahead, Put Others First
20. Teachability: To Keep Leading, Keep Learning
21. Vision: You Can Seize Only What You Can See

Although this is a book primarily targeted for the business market (with over a million copies sold), notice how the leadership traits listed are so similar to the traits listed previously for Army leaders and Navy leaders.

Finally, no list on leadership traits could be complete without a reference to arguably the greatest leader of the twentieth century, Winston Churchill. In Hayward's *Churchill on Leadership,* Sir Winston's personal leadership traits are listed as follows:

- Courage and Optimism
- Kindness, Magnanimity, and Gratitude
- Independent Judgment and Self-Criticism
- Loyalty to the Team

- Rest, Relaxation, and Change of Pace
- Calmness under Stress
- Personal Contact with Subordinates
- Ability to Face Bad News Squarely and Candidly

If we did all the things we were capable of doing, we would literally astound ourselves. . . . Many of life's failures are people who did not realize how close they were to success when they gave up.

—*Thomas A. Edison*

As you can see, there are many ways of looking at traits and characteristics. None are exactly the same, but there are enough commonalities to give you a clear picture of what the real leader should be. In chapter 10, as you build your own leadership development plan, we'll ask you to list what you think are the traits *you* view as necessary for a leader. But before then, let's move past leadership traits (what leaders *are*), and move on to what leaders *do*—their competencies.

WHAT LEADERS DO: COMPETENCIES

Remember, we're summarizing thirty-five leadership books, representing ten thousand pages and hundreds of lists about leadership. In the previous section we reviewed what they provided as the traits of leadership. But they also described leadership in terms of competencies—that's what we'll look at now.

Again, let's look at the seagoing viewpoint, then the view from other military services, and then the view from business and academia.

Nearly all men can stand adversity, but if you want to test a man's character, give him power.

—*Abraham Lincoln*

In the textbook *Fundamentals of Naval Leadership,* produced by the Department of Leadership and Law at the Naval Academy, the following list of leadership competencies is provided. According to the text, an effective leader

- sets the example
- has learned to be a good follower
- knows his job
- establishes objectives and plans for their accomplishment
- knows himself and seeks self-improvement
- takes responsibility for his actions, regardless of their outcome
- is consistent, but not inflexible
- seeks responsibility
- develops a sense of responsibility among his subordinates
- treats every person as an individual, not a number
- keeps his subordinates informed
- encourages subordinates to offer suggestions and constructive criticism
- makes sure the task is understood, supervised, and accomplished
- trains his subordinates as a team
- employs his unit in accordance with its capabilities.

The *Division Officers Guide* bills itself as "A Handbook for Junior Officers and Petty Officers in the U.S. Navy and the U.S. Coast Guard." Coauthored by ADM James Stavridis, it's a great book for any young seagoing officer. It lists five primary leadership competencies for the young leader:

1. Communication
2. Supervision
3. Teaching and counseling

4. Team development
5. Personal competencies

⚓

The sage senior officers in *Naval Leadership: Voices of Experience* collectively view eight major steps to mission accomplishment. That makes them required competencies for any officer who wants to be effective. They are:

1. Know the Job
2. Plan the Mission
3. Implement the Plan
4. Monitor Progress
5. Motivate
6. Maintain Morale
7. Make Things Happen through People
8. Provide Training

Hereafter, if you should observe an occasion to give your officers and friends a little more praise than is their due, and confess more fault than you can justly be charged with, you will only become the sooner for it, a great captain.

—*Benjamin Franklin, letter to John Paul Jones*

⚓

The Department of Defense, through the National Defense University, publishes *The Armed Forces Officer*, which describes the following five leadership competencies:

1. Leadership is a bond of trust.
2. Leaders set and enforce the standards.
3. Leaders set the example.
4. Leaders model courage, both physical and moral.
5. Leaders build and sustain morale.

⚓

Charles Garcia graduated from the Air Force Academy and served as an officer before being selected for the prestigious White House Fellows program. He studied White House Fellows and the leaders they worked for and wrote the book *Leadership Lessons of the White House Fellows.* He devotes a chapter to each of twenty primary leadership competencies:

1. Leaders Know There's More to Life Than Work.
2. Leaders Focus on the Mission.
3. Leaders Have a Laserlike Focus on Their People.
4. Leaders Root Out Prejudice in Themselves and Others.
5. Leaders Act with Integrity.
6. Leaders Create a Sense of Urgency.
7. Leaders Have Passion.
8. Leaders Are Persistent.
9. Leaders Are Great Communicators.
10. Leaders Ask the Tough Questions That Need to Be Asked.
11. Leaders Take Risks.
12. Leaders Understand That Not Every Battle Is the End of the War.
13. Leaders Energize Their People.
14. Leaders Are Great Listeners.
15. Leaders Are Persuasive.
16. Leaders Know When to Compromise and When to Stand Firm.
17. Leaders Are Problem Solvers.
18. Leaders Lead by Walking Around.
19. Leaders Are Transformational Change Agents.
20. Leaders Lead through Experience and Competence, Not through Title or Position.

The civilians of the Department of Homeland Security (DHS) are led by members of the Senior Executive Service (SES). They're equivalent in rank to generals and admirals among federal government workers. DHS has defined eight "Core Leadership Competencies" that it wants these federal leaders to demonstrate, and each SES member is rated each year against these competencies. It's a fabulous description of senior leadership in a complex organization. DHS wants each of its leaders to be:

1. Principled—adheres to the highest ethical standards of public service and integrity
2. People-Centered—engages, values, motivates, mentors, recruits, clearly directs, and appropriately rewards employees
3. Effective Communicator—defines the mission with clarity; listens effectively; shares information
4. Performance-Centered—establishes and meets clear and meaningful goals; uses good judgment in decision making
5. A Diversity Advocate—promotes workforce diversity; provides equitable recognition and equal opportunity; addresses allegations of harassment or discrimination
6. Highly Collaborative—partners effectively within and across DHS components and with external state, local, and international partners
7. Nimble and Innovative—brings creative discipline to encourage continuous innovation
8. A Steward of Public Resources—ensures financial and managerial accountability; takes care of financial and information resources

On a more business-oriented note, Personnel Decisions International Corporation published the *Successful Executive's Handbook,* which identifies twenty-two specific leadership skill sets, grouped into eight primary competencies. Take a look!

1. Thinking
   - Seasoned Judgment
   - Visionary Thinking
   - Financial Acumen
   - Global Perspective
2. Strategic Management
   - Shaping Strategy
   - Driving Execution
3. Leadership
   - Attracting and Developing Talent
   - Empowering Others
   - Influencing and Negotiating
   - Leadership Versatility

There is nothing brilliant or outstanding in my record, except perhaps this one thing: I do the things that I believe ought to be done. . . . And when I make up my mind to do a thing, I act.

—*Theodore Roosevelt*

---

4. Interpersonal
   - Building Organizational Relationships
   - Inspiring Trust
5. Communication
   - High-Impact Delivery
   - Fostering Open Dialogue
6. Motivation
   - Entrepreneurial Risk Taking
   - Drive for Stakeholder Success

7. Self-Management
   – Career and Self-Direction
   – Adaptability
   – Mature Confidence
8. Breadth and Depth
   – Business Situation Versatility
   – Industry Knowledge
   – Cross-Functional Capability

Similarly, the American Management Association published *The AMA Handbook of Leadership.* In the chapter "What Is an Effective Leader?" the authors list five rules and four overarching competencies for leaders.

The five rules are:

1. Shape the future. Leaders must strategize the future they intend to create.
2. Make things happen. Leaders must execute.
3. Engage today's talent. Leaders must build strong teams.
4. Build the next generation. Leaders must develop today's human capital into tomorrow's team leaders.
5. Invest in yourself. Leaders must learn their job and their craft as a leader.

The four general observations on competencies are:

1. All leaders must excel at personal proficiency.
2. All leaders must have one towering strength.
3. Each leader must be at least average in his or her "weaker" leadership domains.
4. Leaders must be able to grow.

Speaking of business books, you've no doubt seen the plethora of books that begin with "Leadership Lessons of X," or "X on Leadership." The "Xs" include Gandhi, John Wooden, John F. Kennedy, Rudy Giuliani, Shakespeare, General Zinni, Irwin Rommel, Tony Soprano, Moses, Robert E. Lee, Churchill, Patton, Attila the Hun, Lincoln, and on and on.

One of the many books of this genre is *The Leadership Lessons of Jesus*. It includes the following list of leadership competencies:

1. Leaders call followers.
2. Leaders teach with authority.
3. Leaders take care of their people.
4. Leadership requires discipline.
5. Leaders expect the unexpected.
6. Leaders eat with the troops.
7. Leaders usc traditions.
8. Leaders plan.
9. Leaders tell stories.
10. Leaders are faithful.
11. Leaders are visible.
12. Leaders take decisive action.

It is very important that officers realize that they are being observed at all times, and they should conduct themselves properly not only on the job, but also when they are on liberty or anywhere else. [For the crew,] . . . an officer's misbehavior is most often a topic of conversation.

—*Master Chief Petty Officer of the Navy Sanders*

On a more academic note, the postgraduate textbook *The Nature of Leadership* provides two excellent lists of leadership skills, based on an overview of academic literature on the subject. This may be the most comprehensive and useful list available. Use it to measure yourself in chapter 10 to follow!

Basic Leadership Skills	Advanced Leadership Skills
Learning from Experience	Delegating
Communication	Managing Conflict
Listening	Negotiation
Assertiveness	Problem Solving
Providing Constructive Feedback	Improving Creativity
Effective Stress Management	Diagnosing Performance Problems
Technical Competence	Team Building
Effective Relationships with Superiors	Building High-Performance Teams
Effective Relationships with Peers	Development Planning
Setting Goals	Credibility
Punishment	Coaching
Conducting Meetings	Empowerment

So, do you have a sense of the ten or fifteen traits that you want to establish **within yourself** as a leader? Do you have another dozen skills or competencies you feel you need to develop? Great! In chapter 6, we'll look at a new set of lists—lists of advice from older, wiser writers to young budding leaders like you. In the meantime, though, let's hear some sea stories in leadership.

CHAPTER 3

Sea Stories in Leadership

Our recent research has led us to conclude that one of the most reliable indicators and predictors of true leadership is an individual's ability to find meaning in negative events and to learn from even the most trying circumstances.

. . .

It is the combination of hardiness and ability to grasp context that, above all, allows a person to not only survive an ordeal, but to learn from it, and to emerge stronger, more engaged, and more committed than ever.

. . .

These attributes allow leaders to grow from their crucibles, instead of being destroyed by them—to find opportunity where others might find only despair.

. . .

This is the stuff of true leadership.

—Warren Bennis and Robert Thomas

As a young officer I had to endure my fair share of classroom training, both ashore and afloat. I read the articles and heard the lectures and studied the books. Some of that training was in leadership.

But the lessons I remember are those that were told to me by real people who had been there. Today, thirty years later, I can close my eyes and recall sea stories that illustrated lessons learned by others. And, in recalling and retelling the stories, I learn the lessons again.

Jesus told stories, or parables, to teach lessons. So did Buddha and Abraham Lincoln. They told them because they work. If it's good enough for them, it's good enough for me.

So, to that end, this chapter provides a handful of sea stories told by seagoing seniors. Chapter 7 contains a few more. Reading them might not be as good as hearing them in person, but please give them a look, and try to internalize the hard-won lessons they represent.

PRAISING IN PUBLIC

One of the enduring principles of leadership is that you praise in public and criticize or rebuke in private. As the following sea story illustrates, failure to adhere to this principle can have unintended consequences. In June 1972 I reported as chief engineer to a *Knox*-class destroyer escort (DE) just prior to its first deployment of any kind, this one being a deployment to Vietnam. That deployment went exceptionally well; the ship earned a very positive reputation, and the captain, who had joined the ship en route to WESTPAC, was highly regarded by the crew (an important point for the purpose of this story). In late summer of 1973 the ship was assigned as part of a carrier screen during a deployment to the Mediterranean. Somewhere about mid-Atlantic on a sunny morning with an extremely tranquil sea, a leak developed in a flange of the high-pressure steam line going to the main engine. The flange was located just outside the main control portside door where it posed a very serious safety hazard to personnel. The captain was duly notified; he then notified the admiral of the problem and that we were going to have to go dead in the water (DIW). The unrealistic hope and plan as conveyed to the admiral was that we would let the system cool down for 60–90 minutes and then torque the flange bolts in hopes that the leak would stop. This plan was carried out, we started to build steam to the engine, and, as not unexpected, the flange still leaked. We dutifully notified the admiral of this and that we had no alternative but to go DIW again and let the system cool down enough that we could replace the flange seal without risking warping of the new seal (only one replacement was carried). We gave the admiral an estimate of six hours without really having any idea of what the time would really be.

During all this repair time the carrier and its screen circled us. It was definitely not the kind of visibility that the crew of a ship wants regardless of rank or rate. After about four hours we decided to attempt the replacement. That process was relatively fast, after which we began to slowly elevate the flange temperature. After an elapsed time of about four and a half hours, we notified the bridge that we were ready to answer all bells. With that the captain ordered me via the squawk box to report to the bridge. I reported to the bridge fully expecting a dressing-down but also expecting that the captain would ask me to follow him to his stateroom. Instead, in front of the bridge watch he began to give me a profanity-laced tongue-lashing that was worse than I could have imagined. He screamed that I had embarrassed him, the ship, and the crew before the task group and had made us the laughingstock of the Navy. For the better part of what seemed like five minutes he hurled profanity-laced invectives at me and, by extension, my engineers. During the whole episode the bridge watch team had the most uncomfortable look on their faces. You could tell that everyone just wanted to evaporate.

Admonish your friends in private; praise them in public.

—*Publilius Syrus, 50 BC*

There is no telling how long the captain's tirade might have gone on, but it was interrupted by the admiral calling the captain over the primary tactical circuit, which happened to be patched to the speaker on the bridge. The admiral proceeded to tell the captain (and everyone on the bridge) that he wanted his verbal commendation passed along to the engineers for doing in four and a half hours what the carrier's chief engineer had said would take six to seven hours. The admiral's call, which probably lasted about a minute, was nothing short of effusive in its praise. After the admiral signed off, you could have heard a pin drop. The captain said nothing, getting out of his chair in a glaring rage and departing for his stateroom. After his departure, the bridge watch offered me its congratulations, and by mealtime the bridge "scene" was a legend on the mess deck. The point of this story is that the captain destroyed in five minutes the esteem that he had earned from the crew in the previous year. He never regained that esteem, all because he forgot the principle of praise in public, rebuke in private.

—*LCDR Jeffrey Belden, USN*

WAKING UP THE SKIPPER

As an ensign, I quickly qualified as a deck watch officer (DWO) during my first patrol on a Coast Guard cutter. During this patrol, our unit was operating in the Windward Passage between Cuba and Haiti. During one of my first 0400–0800 watches as a qualified DWO, the commanding officer (CO) came up to the bridge following his wake-up call. Upon arriving on the bridge, the CO noticed the beautiful sunrise over the mountains of Haiti off in the distance. I was immediately lectured by the skipper on my insensitivity for selfishly enjoying the sunrise by myself, and I was instructed that in the future I was to let the CO know whenever there was a nice sunrise. With only three qualified DWOs, I again had the 0400–0800 the next morning and again, another picture-perfect sunrise was getting ready to occur over Haiti. Remembering the proverbial butt chewing I received the day before, I was at a decision point. The sunrise was going to occur approximately ten minutes before the CO's scheduled wake-up call per the night orders book. I was very confident that the CO was merely having fun at my expense the day before. Therefore, should I wake up the skipper early or follow his night orders?

Every man is the architect of his own fortune.

—*Gaius Sallustius Crispus*

In the end, I phoned the CO early, identified myself as the officer of the deck, told him what time it was and that all was quiet on the bridge but that a lovely sunrise was fixing to occur in a few minutes over Haiti. I received a "Very well Mr. Tomney, thank you" in response. The remaining hour or so of the watch remained quiet, and I was relieved about 0730 and headed to the wardroom for breakfast. When I arrived, the CO was already there. The skipper looked over to me, smiled, and said, "Touché." He never again asked to be awakened for a sunrise. While I was confident that my CO was having some fun with me on one of my first morning watches, I did receive a "verbal order" to notify him of any future sunrises. While it would have been easy to have simply followed the night orders book the next morning, I felt that as a junior officer, I too could have some fun with the CO. If anything, I felt the CO could learn to count on me for being responsive to his words and trustworthy enough to call him for even the most mundane issues. The fact that I got some small satisfaction from waking the CO was icing on the cake!

—*RDML Christopher Tomney, USCG*

THE VALUE OF SECOND CHANCES

In 1995 my first ship, the USS *Barney* (DDG-6), was in a dry dock in Norfolk, Virginia, making post-deployment repairs. I had joined the ship two months earlier in the Arabian Gulf. Assigned as the antisubmarine warfare (ASW) officer, I was consumed that week getting my team trained and certified at the ASW Trainers. While at the trainer I received an urgent phone call that a hurricane was heading for a direct hit on Norfolk and the dry dock had already started flooding. I rushed back to the ship. My most important task was to pressurize our two rubber sonar domes. My chief sonar technician supervised the work; I looked on for hours not knowing much about how the system worked. We screwed it up badly. A few days later we learned we had done extensive damage to the sonar transducers and dome structure. A major dry docking was required to effect repairs.

A formal Judge Advocate General (JAG) investigation ensued and resulted in my receiving a Non-Punitive Letter of Caution. I had failed in my duties in many ways. I did not pay attention to the deteriorating weather conditions and the impact on my ship. I failed to use operational risk management (ORM) and develop a contingency plan prior to going into dry dock. I failed to properly supervise a critical evolution for which I was responsible regardless of my lack of knowledge or training. I did not know how my equipment worked. The results of the investigation hit me hard—I was absolutely certain my career was over.

You may make mistakes, but you are not a failure
until you start blaming someone else.

—Unknown

Years later I realized just how wise and patient my captain had been. He gave me a non-punitive letter, worked on my shortfalls, and eventually developed me into a competent Surface Warrior. This captain gave me a second chance and it changed my life. Your Sailors are human beings and will also make mistakes; be generous with those second chances, and do your best to develop their full potential!

—*RDML Brian L. LaRoche, USN*

THE BIRD-CAGED WIRE

During one of my first tours on a ship after graduation from a maritime academy, I was in charge of the aft gang as we were preparing to tie up the 50,000-ton oil tanker to the Christy Lee, an oil platform near the entrance to Drift River, Cook Inlet, Alaska. It was the middle of winter; the temperature was below zero and the current was roaring through. During that time of year, two pilots were maintained on board to stand a radar watch on the bridge, looking for ice floes that could force us away from the rig and part our lines. During the previous undocking evolution, the mooring wire was improperly stowed on the drum. As we began to pay out the wire, it bird-caged on the drum and became wedged within itself. It was dangling in the water. We could no longer pay out or haul in the wire. We tried several times to free it using our usual methods. After several minutes, I radioed up to the captain and told him that we couldn't get it loose. What he said to me was simple yet true, "Mate, you *have* to get it loose."

> No one is thinking if everyone is thinking alike.
>
> —*GEN George S. Patton*

That line was essential to the safe and effective mooring of the vessel, given the current. There was no workaround. In these conditions, the only way to complete the evolution was to safely free up that wire and make that piece of equipment work. The captain made it perfectly clear to everyone who was listening. After some more time, with some experienced seamen and ingenuity, we freed the wire and were able to tie up properly and safely. This was my first experience being challenged by a problem seemingly so simple, yet so integral to the operation.

Moral: It taught me that there is value in every detail of the operation and that sometimes there are problems that need to be solved immediately and with a sense of urgency. Sometimes you just have to make it happen, *and* keep everyone safe.

—*2nd Mate Aaron Asimakopoulos,*
Merchant Mariner and Navy Reservist

RAISING STANDARDS

I joined an *Aegis*-class cruiser as the executive officer (XO) while it was on deployment; it didn't take long for me to figure out that there was room for improvement. The passageways were dirty and dingy, brass wasn't shined, fire stations weren't properly stowed, papers were taped up to bulkheads, and so forth. And as I started doing daily messing and berthing inspections, I found the berthing compartments and heads to be dirty, racks not made, and gear adrift. So, taking a page from the "start hard" playbook, I got the department heads and command master chief together and told them the ship was UNSAT and they were going to help me get it squared away. I started formal passageway inspections, with each space presented by the Sailor who owned it, with the divisional chief petty officer and division officer present.

Damn the torpedoes; full speed ahead!

—*ADM David Farragut*

These were very tough inspections to a very high standard: perfect cleanliness, brass shined, everything perfectly stowed, all damage control gear in place and properly stowed, watertight doors perfectly maintained, and so on. I would inspect the ship in sections to keep the duration reasonable while allowing time for a detailed assessment. When a day's inspection was over, I would get on the ship's general announcing system (the 1MC) and announce the "Best Passageway" winner, "Best Shined Brass" winner, and other awards, giving credit to the division and department and often the individual Sailor who owned the space. The results were instantaneous and dramatic. Within a month the ship shined and department heads, division officers, chiefs, and petty officers were trying to outdo each other in the "Best Space" competition.

I did the same thing for berthing compartments, with the same results. Once I had the ship up to that standard, it stayed that way for my entire twenty-month tour. The lesson is: start out strong, set high standards, insist that people meet your standards, and find positive ways to motivate and incentivize your people.

—*RADM Kevin Quinn, USN*

BREAKING THE GENDER BARRIER AT DIVE SCHOOL

In November 1979 I reported to the Navy School of Diving and Salvage in Washington, D.C. Diving and salvage was considered one of the more challenging pursuits for a newly commissioned ensign; I was one of the first three women to attend diving school. The Mark V diving rig weighed 198 pounds, and the mixed gas rig weighed a whopping 300 pounds. And, of course, a school that starts in November and graduates in May in Washington, D.C., translates into a long winter of diving and tending in the cold, icy Anacostia River. On the first day of school, Chief Youngblood met me with a roar, barking out, "I bet you don't last a week in this school and I'll make sure you don't." I accepted that bet. For a week he took great pleasure in riding me during long morning physical training sessions and seemingly endless runs to the pool. By the end of the week, I had had enough and snapped back. But as we all know, students don't have the right to yell at an instructor. I paid dearly with a massive number of penalty push-ups and eight-count body builders, but I had made it to the end of the week and did not quit. The chief paid off his bet with a smile and said, "I knew you would make it."

Genius is 1 percent inspiration, and 99 percent perspiration.

—*Thomas Edison*

The chief probably singled me out because the diving school was unaccustomed to women students, at a time when the Navy was still "adjusting" to new opportunities that had been opened to women. His attitude infuriated me to success. However, the real leadership lesson occurred in the twenty-two weeks that followed. He invested his time and energies in teaching and mentoring me to ensure I could meet the requirements of the school. He invested in the human resource and recognized the capability that could be cultivated. At times it meant coming in on the weekends to do extra work, but he invested himself in the effort. To this impressionable ensign, he showed that leadership is about selfless devotion to duty and a willingness to invest in the success of others. Whether he agreed with women entering his world of "Navy Diver" was unimportant; he encouraged excellence and commitment because it was the right thing to do, regardless of my gender.

—*RDML Martha Herb, USN*

HOT AND COLD

When I was a midshipman, we had a company officer who ran hot and cold. He was a lieutenant commander (LCDR). Sometimes he was the nicest guy you'd ever meet—he'd fool around with us, he was one of the gang, he'd tell jokes, he'd cut us slack. We loved that guy.

But on some days, maybe 25 percent of the time, he was mean and cranky. He'd snap at you for no reason. He'd inspect the rooms and yell at us for things that had been fine the week before. We'd see him coming down the passageway and we'd get out of his way if we could. We hated that guy.

> Officers of inharmonious disposition, irrespective of their ability, must be removed. A staff cannot function properly unless it is a united family.
>
> —GEN George S. Patton

And the problem was that we could never tell which guy he would be. It was really hard to work with him, to submit requests, to get decisions, to seek advice and counseling. Because we'd like the nice guy but be afraid of the mean guy.

Then he transferred out and was replaced by a Marine Corps captain. He was a hard-ass. He'd never fool around with us; he wasn't part of the gang; he never cut us slack. On the other hand, he'd never snap at us for no reason. He was consistent in every way. He never raised his voice, either in laughter or in irritation. He took a steady strain. He had high standards—higher than the LCDR's—and he insisted we maintain them. While the LCDR was up and down, high and low, hot and cold, the Marine was constant. You always knew what he'd be like, and where you stood with him. You could count on it.

And you know what? Even though originally we were bummed out that our friendly but inconsistent LCDR had been replaced by this butt-kicking Marine, after a while the company really began to blossom. We actually performed better. We could count on him and depend on him. That first year he was there, we ended up winning the Color Competition as the best company of the thirty-six companies.

In the thirty years since then, I've always remembered that story. I try to be consistent, to let my people depend on me. I try not to raise my voice or to let my own issues affect my demeanor. I owe it to my people to give them the solid constancy and predictability they deserve to excel.

—*RADM Robert Wray, USN*

PRESENTATION MATTERS

Zone inspections are a critical part of the good order and discipline on any ship. As a division officer in the mid-1980s, my initial tours were topside, as fire control officer, gunnery officer, and electronic warfare officer.

When a new commanding officer (CO) arrived, he decided to move junior officers around—topside division officers would move below decks and below-deck division officers would move topside. For me, this meant I would join the snipes in the engineering department, as the auxiliaries officer. Our division responsibilities included such non-sexy equipment as the anchor windlass, fire pumps, steering gear, air compressors, evaporators, refrigeration units, water heaters, potable water pumps, and the ship's small boats.

Our captain held zone inspections each week. It was easier to prepare for weekly zone inspections in my topside division officer tours. For example, the radar rooms and compartments in the fire control division were always very clean, organized, and air-conditioned. The equipment was new and almost always worked as designed. The Sailors were all well trained, and the billets were generally all filled.

In contrast, the auxiliary division was not as well manned and was in port-and-starboard watches. It was a challenge and took quite bit of effort to keep multiple auxiliary spaces (pump rooms, reefer decks, and after steering) as shipshape and as good looking as a topside radar rooms.

Because of the type of equipment and talented and well-trained Sailors, the combat systems department almost always won CO's zone inspection contest for best division. The engineering department never won. With my new assignment, I was stubborn and competitive enough to want to change that record.

We were deploying again. Before we left, I told the division of my plan to go after the brass ring—to win zone inspections. At the time, I don't think they believed we would succeed, but they promised their support.

The transit from Norfolk to the Persian Gulf was plagued with bad weather, so zone inspections were halted for a couple of weeks. This was the break the division needed. This was our opportunity.

We took that time to repair equipment, do planned maintenance, clean, paint, and ready our auxiliary spaces for our first zone inspection under my tutelage. When not on watch, I worked right alongside the enginemen to complete maintenance, clean, chip, and paint. At the end of more than two weeks of extraordinary effort, our compartments looked outstanding. But they were still far from looking like the clean, air-conditioned radar rooms topside.

> Getting good players is easy.
> Gettin' 'em to play together is the hard part.
>
> —*Casey Stengel*

We needed a "Plan B." Despite the hard work we invested in readying our equipment and compartments, it was clear we were also going to need our "presentation" of the spaces to be equally on target.

Our CO was small in stature—maybe five feet six inches. So, to present our spaces during the inspection, we strategically chose a tall six-foot-three-inch engineman who had only been in the Navy a couple of years. He was from the Bronx in New York City and had worked as a used-car salesman before he entered the Navy.

Before the inspection, the chief and I briefed him on how to present each space. He was to meet the captain outside each compartment and escort him throughout the space. We coached him to stay very close and in front of the captain, facing him at all times, and to talk to him as loud and fast as he possibly could. Because the young engineman was so tall and the captain much smaller, the captain was forced to look up at the engineman's face during the inspection. This was just what I wanted—to distract the captain from looking down at the equipment. By looking up, the captain was not able to spend a lot of time looking around the spaces.

When the four-hour ship-wide inspection was completed, the captain got on the general announcing system and announced the winner—the best division on the ship. As we waited in great anticipation the word finally came: the auxiliaries division and the A-gang Sailors won! We were all proud of our accomplishment that day. We were prepared, our equipment worked, we worked hard—but we needed an edge and our tall New Yorker provided it.

In the months that followed, the other divisions worked hard to try to beat us, but once we had the division at such a high standard (and with our special presentation), we stayed at the top for the rest of the deployment.

The moral of the story: despite hard work, presentation matters!

—*RADM Chris Paul, USN*

DELIVERING BAD NEWS

As a lieutenant, I was the assistant navigator on an aircraft carrier, getting ready to go into the shipyard for about three months. I was tasked to oversee the entire crew's work package; I was responsible for all the work the crew would do on the ship during this period. The captain had a reputation for a quick temper but was universally regarded as an outstanding commander and officer.

Before the shipyard period, the captain called a meeting in his stateroom for the other officers who would play a major role in this maintenance period. Each of the other officers, all very senior to me, gave their reports stating that all the work would get done and that it would be the best shipyard period ever. When he got to me, I told him I was very concerned that each department, particularly engineering, had bitten off more than they could chew. I presented a list of over one thousand items that Repair Division said they would do in the coming three months. I told the captain that I had doubts as to whether this could be done, and that I'd work with the repair officer to prioritize what needed to be completed.

He glared at me and I thought I was in trouble. He then faced the other, more senior officers and said that this was exactly what he wanted to hear. While not doubting any of the other reports, he stated that if we had bad news, then he wanted to hear it! He would rather know ahead of time than be surprised in the end. He demanded total honesty from us all and never once shot the messenger. This made the whole shipyard experience a pleasant one for me professionally, and for the ship in general.

Lessons I learned: First, give your bosses bad news, even if you think they won't like it, because they need to get it to do their job. And second, if you want your folks to give you the bad news you need to know to do your job, don't shoot the messenger! If you do, they won't give you bad news, and that's not good for you or your ship.

—CDR *Ted Kramer, USN*

FORTUNE FAVORS BOLDNESS

As a young division officer I was the main propulsion assistant (MPA) and Boilers Division officer on a frigate. I had over twenty outstanding and extremely hardworking boiler technicians (BTs). One of our real superstars was a petty officer 1st class (BT1) who was one of our two automatic boiler controls experts ("ABC Techs"). Our BT1 was the greatest and our new captain knew it.

While getting ready for our operational propulsion plant exam (OPPE), a tough exam that would reflect greatly on our non-engineering–background captain, we maintained our plant and trained our watchstanders relentlessly.

As we prepared to go to sea one final week to run engineering drills before the OPPE, our superstar BT1 approached me with a leave request. Like most ships, our policy was that you didn't ask for non-emergency leave when we were going to be at sea. But our superstar's young wife was due to deliver their first child that week we would be at sea, and he "really wanted, really needed" to be there.

The boilers were controlled automatically by a mechanically complex system of low-pressure "control air." We knew that an important drill during the OPPE would be "Loss of Control Air." The BT1 owned this system; his potential absence meant that if we had a real control air casualty we could not fix ourselves at sea, we would miss our last chance to practice that critical drill before the OPPE.

Understandably the chief engineer, executive officer, and captain thought the BT1 needed to be at sea doing his critical job and that his wife would be fine there in San Diego, if she did deliver that week. The BT1 was devastated and protested that his backup, a younger Sailor (a BT2) was qualified to do the job. Being young myself and not fully appreciating the professional pressure my superiors were facing, I decided to go back up the chain of command and plead the case directly to the captain.

The captain, to his credit, said, "Alright, MPA, we'll leave BT1 behind but you had better hope those ABCs work, or else!"

So we left BT1 behind. During the first set of drills at sea, naturally, we sustained an actual control air casualty. Our frigate went dead in the water (DIW) and began rolling heavily. The BT2, under pressure, dove in and fixed the problem! And it turned out that BT2 was a true ABC genius whose talent had never been known because BT1 was so good.

That Friday afternoon as we came alongside the pier, BT1 was waiting, smiling broadly and holding his new child in his arms. As the brow was opened BT1 handed his tiny new baby to his wife and bounded back aboard like a man possessed. He spent every remaining minute before the exam grooming his ABCs to the point he was polishing the control air lines themselves! And BT2 was right alongside him, inspired by his recent "victory at sea." Together they delivered; the examining team said it was "the best ABC system they had ever seen."

It was only the first of many times in my career leading Sailors that, when I accepted risk to my success for their benefit, I was rewarded beyond what I could have imagined. Leadership lesson: If you take care of the Sailors, they will take care of the ship . . . and you!

—*RADM John Christenson, USN*

WHEN THINGS GO BAD, LOOK IN THE MIRROR

Sometimes when things are bad, you need to step back and take a hard look at yourself. Many years ago, we were under way for a tactical inspection on my first submarine. I was an experienced LT, selected to stand watch as officer of the deck (OOD). We were on the surface transiting to the dive point. A request came to the bridge that sounded a little funny, so I asked a follow-up question. I did not like the answer, so the request was denied. A few minutes later the request came in again, but this time as direction from the XO. A little while later another request came in, only this time it appeared to directly contradict something I had been told to consider as part of the inspection. Once again I denied the request. Shortly after that, my relief told me that I would be rigging the bridge for dive and that he would relieve me later. This meant I had an extra two hours on watch. I was unamused. As I recall, every request that came to the bridge after that seemed more and more inappropriate.

> The true leader must submerge himself
> in the fountain of the people.
>
> —*V. I. Lenin*

Sometime later, not long I am sure, the XO came to the bridge. I never forgot the conversation. He looked around the bridge. Great weather operating out of Hawaii. "How's it going?" I should have detected the tone of his voice, but I commenced venting instead. "Everyone down there (below decks) is screwed up! They keep asking for all these stupid things, making ridiculous requests! It's unbelievable!" He nodded. "When everyone is pissing you off, it ain't them." I looked at him, speechless. "For the rest of your watch, you will do whatever they ask." He paused. "Any questions?" This time the tone was clear. "No, sir." He smiled. "Good, have a good watch!" He was serious, and he went below decks.

I have never forgotten that advice. So when it seems everyone is screwing up I go away and think very carefully about what is really happening. And if the problem is everyone, you need to look in a mirror.

—*CAPT Scott Minium, USN*

COMMAND-ADVANCING A SAILOR

The Command Advancement Program (CAP) allows a ship's CO to promote or advance a Sailor, even if he or she hasn't achieved test scores high enough for regular advancement. This is the story of the most memorable command advancement I ever saw. . . .

A boatswain's mate 2nd class (BM2) had taken the test to be advanced to first class at least a dozen times and had passed the test, but hadn't achieved high enough scores to be advanced. He was a recognized leader in his division, department, and on the ship. He had qualified officer of the deck (under way) and was by all accounts performing well above his pay grade. The Command Advancement board met and the decision was easy.

The superior man is firm in the right way, and not merely firm.

—Confucius

The question was: how to execute the advancement? The most common way is to wait until the results of the latest advancement exam were published and then command-advance the deserving Sailor who passed but didn't get advanced. But I wanted to do something better for this Sailor. So, on the day of the First Class exam all the Second Class were on the mess decks taking the exam. Shortly after it started we mustered the crew on the fantail. We then sent for the BM2 to be pulled out of the exam because there was some catastrophe that only he could deal with on the fantail. Of course, the BM2 hopped right up; after all, the ship needed him! He popped out on the fantail and saw the crew, but still didn't know what was happening.

The captain signaled the BM2 over and asked what he was doing. When he replied that he was taking the advancement exam the CO asked, "Why are you doing that? You're already a BM1!" The crew burst into applause and the BM1 got all choked up. It was a great day for all and a great way to take care of a great Sailor.

—RADM Tom Rowden, USN

PREPARATION, AND SOMETHING ELSE

After active Navy and Coast Guard duty, my first job with an unlimited tonnage license was as mate and pilot aboard a large excursion steamer. The vessel made daily harbor trips with nine hundred passengers and a large unskilled deck crew of day workers drawn from a nearby housing project at the minimum wage. They were a tough bunch. The lower hull had numerous watertight hatches and doors breaking her watertight bulkheads. I required the crew to patrol the dark, damp, and dirty lower hull before every cruise and close all the watertight hatches and doors. I then went through the hull myself before we got under way. The previous mate had not made the crew do this onerous chore and they didn't like doing it.

One day with most of the deck crew gathered about, the lead deckhand asked me why I required this nasty chore. At that moment we had just finished the lower hull closure patrol and were standing on the main deck looking down at the ladder into the lower hull. I thought a minute, looked around at the gang waiting for my reply, and said: "Shorty, if we don't close all those doors, and we got hit out on the trip, the water would flow through the boat and sink us like a rock. When we close the doors we create watertight compartments and the boat can stay afloat even with some of them flooded. Now, we can either ensure that all the doors are closed each day before we get under way or we'd have to go down there after we got hit. After we get hit it would be completely dark down there and flooding with cold water. You guys wouldn't want to have to go down there. But we would have to go down there. I might have to force some of you down into that dark, flooding place with a gun. Isn't it better that we all get this accomplished together at the dock with the lights on?"

The commander stands for the virtues of wisdom, sincerity, benevolence, courage, and strictness.

—*Sun Tzu*

Not only did the deck crew never ask again why they did this chore, but I never had to remind them again to do it. I think this illustrates the value of one primary leadership requirement for maritime operations: preparation. Oh, and one very important secondary skill: highly imaged motivational speaking!

—CAPT Ray Bollinger, Merchant Mariner,
and former Master Chief Petty Officer

NO DOUBLE STANDARDS

In the summer of 1995, prior to beginning the Quantico phase of Midshipmen Leadership Training for USNA midshipmen, I took the company on a conditioning run (3 miles, 8.5-minute pace formation run). The run was on terrain familiar to all the midshipmen in the company. The summer company of about 160 midshipmen was co-ed, with 26 women. My executive officer (XO) was in the rear of the formation picking up stragglers. At the end of the run, I had 26 drops—every female in the company dropped out of the run. I directed my XO to have all the stragglers stand by in the company office prior to the morning meal formation. He advised against it. I asked why. He replied that the only stragglers were women and it might not look right. I told him that his reasoning was irrelevant.

> Bring me solutions, not problems.
>
> —Margaret Thatcher

I met with the stragglers and asked, "What's wrong with this picture?" One of the women replied, "There's no guys here." I responded as follows: There are a lot of people, both here and graduated from the Academy, that do not feel that women belong at USNA. They believe that the different (lower) physical standards applied to women give them an unfair advantage. The fact that all the women in the company could not finish a three-mile run did nothing to put this perception to rest. I told the women that the run was not hard and that the only reason they did not finish the run was they "believed" they could not finish. If their hearts were in it, their heads would follow. I challenged each of them to finish the run the next day or I would leave any stragglers behind and not take them to Quantico. The next day, all the women finished the run.

Moral: Hold all your people to a high standard, and do *not* lower, modify, or have any special consideration for anyone, regardless of gender or race or background. If someone wants to perform, they will.

—*LCDR Pete Long, USN*

THE SINKING SHIP

It was a cold winter night in the middle of the Mediterranean. About midnight. We received a distress call from a Greek freighter en route to Libya; she was sinking. We sped to her location and found the crew already getting into lifeboats. As their ship slumped lower in the water, we hauled them aboard our Navy cruiser.

We launched a boat to circle the sinking freighter. Her crew had seen the flooding in the engine room—they couldn't find the cause, so they abandoned ship. We Navy engineers were chomping at the bit to go on board, to go below, to find the problem and resolve it. We felt we could save the ship, if the captain would only let us try.

Words are plentiful, but deeds are precious.

—*Lech Wałęsa*

But the captain wouldn't buy it. The Greek crew had already abandoned the ship. The shipping company would be compensated by insurance. The cargo was cement—not too precious to be replaced. He couldn't see risking his crew to save this freighter that nobody else seemed to care about. We young engineers thought he was being a conservative old man; we muttered under our breath that he should let us do our job. We pressed him; he still said no.

As the night went on, we stood by, and we continued to circle the vessel in our gig. Just around dawn, suddenly and without warning, the stricken freighter stood up on one end and plunged into the sea. It happened in a minute or less. If we had been inside, we never would have gotten out. After that, we young engineers were glad that our captain had been as conservative as he had.

I learned three lessons. First, sometimes being conservative is the right thing to do, even if others don't think so. Second, don't risk your people unless it's something worth risking them for. And third, don't underestimate the judgment of the captain!

—RADM Robert Wray, USN

THE SKIPPER IS ALWAYS RIGHT (NOT REALLY!)

I remember that night in late 1985 as if it were yesterday. I was a brand-new LT (jg), with a brand–new skipper. We were pulling into port. I was the sea and anchor conning officer and had a rather impish officer of the deck (OOD). The night was calm—no wind, perfect visibility, and more importantly, nobody on the pier. The skipper was just coming off a three-year tour at the Pentagon and in his own words, "rusty, but ready to proceed with no witnesses." His simply stating this should be an indicator of what a great leader he was and is. As we began our approach, the skipper took the conn and clearly stated that if anything "comes up" that I should take the conn back immediately (another sign of a great leader). Our approach was uneventful and the entire sea and anchor detail was at ease despite having the skipper driving.

He that won't be counseled can't be helped.

—*Benjamin Franklin*

As we made our final lineup on the pier, the radio blared that we were to shift to a new berth; this would now force us to dock between the rocky quay wall and another ship preparing to get under way in the early morning. Not too tricky, but enough changes in a short time span to force some critical calculations to be completed quickly. The first approach was very short. The second attempt was a little slower, but didn't get us close enough. Unfortunately at this point the tension was rising just because the skipper was trying so hard and just not landing it. He stayed positive, cracked a couple jokes, and backed us out again. By now I had great situational awareness and had so many sea and anchor details on board that I could have done it with my eyes shut. My mind flashed a thought, "do I offer a couple tips about the ship's handling, or just keep quiet?"

Then the most unexpected thing happened. The skipper asked me what he was doing wrong! The bridge erupted in smiles, all tension was gone, and I felt more at ease to offer suggestions. I told him it takes a while after a long break and that it was a tricky approach. I recommended he leave the speed up a little longer just so we had some steerageway as we cut it. Not surprisingly he heeded my advice, and on the next approach I had to recommend that he slow down a little bit. He did, and his confidence increased as we just missed the perfect landing. The skipper had one more shot in him and he knew this would be it. Unfortunately the "bubble" was lost during the final backing out and the skipper got a little rattled. As we made the final approach, he wanted to make certain he had enough speed to land it. As we completed the backing he adjusted speed up just a little too much and the jagged rocks were now approaching too fast. I looked at the skipper and with just critical seconds remaining, he simply looked at me, nodded, and stepped back. I immediately announced I had the conn, ordered "emergency back full" and "right full rudder." We avoided the rocks, docked, and took a deep breath. Then I mockingly called up Engineering to cancel the divers for the hull inspection. There was silence until the skipper chuckled, smacked me on the back, and the crew finally exhaled.

The safe docking of the ship is not the moral of the story. It is the skipper creating an atmosphere of trial and demonstrating to the crew that it was acceptable for them to do the same in their workspace, with similar safeguards. It taught me and everyone else on the bridge that night to fully understand all situations and speak up when things are turning perilous.

—*RDML Scott Jerabek, USN*

THE AFTERMATH OF THE PARTY

As a lieutenant, I was the commanding officer (CO) of a Coast Guard Island-class 110-foot patrol boat (WPB). During the end of an inport period, our sixteen-member crew (minus me and the XO) held an off-base party that spiraled out of control. Before the evening was done, I had crewmembers who were assaulted, several others who committed underage drinking or contributed by allowing underage drinking, and one crewmember who was arrested for driving while intoxicated. Our unit was preparing for a thirty-day patrol to Haiti and was due to depart our homeport in only three days. My XO hastily completed an investigation so we could dispose of any charges before the deployment.

> It feels painful and scary—that's real delegation.
>
> —*Caspian Woods*

The day we were to leave on patrol, I held Captain's Mast on four crewmembers at 1000. The rest of the crew served either as mast representatives or as witnesses to the various offenses. The four non-judicial punishment proceedings concluded around 1300. We were scheduled to depart that evening from Naval Station Roosevelt Roads, Puerto Rico, at 2000 in order to make our arrival time in Guantanamo Bay, Cuba. The events of the past seventy-two hours were a mental strain on our entire crew, myself included. I felt a nighttime outbound transit was riskier than normal with a crew whose collective thoughts might not had been focused on safe navigation. I elected to contact my O-6 boss in San Juan and requested a twelve-hour delay in sailing until 0800 the following morning. My request was approved.

I learned three lessons from this. First, while it would have been simpler due to the breadth of the disciplinary infractions and our upcoming patrol to merely lecture the crew on their personal responsibilities, I learned that each member had to be held accountable for his actions, even if it was uncomfortable for me to provide that accountability. Second, I also learned that as CO, if my head wasn't completely focused on the upcoming task at hand (night transit), I shouldn't put my ship or crew needlessly at risk. We were all able to get a good night of sleep, clear our collective cobwebs, and depart port the next morning safely in daylight. By slightly adjusting our transit speed we were still able to arrive for relief on time. And third, I learned that everyone should clearly articulate to their supervisor if they are not 100 percent capable of carrying out their duties for any reason.

I am proud to report that in the more than one year I had remaining on my tour, I had no further problems with alcohol by the crew and no additional Captain's Masts.

—*RDML Christopher Tomney, USCG*

CHALLENGE YOUR FOLKS

Many years ago I was in a position of supervising a seaman who was temporarily assigned as a reporter on the ship's newspaper. Since he was very interested in writing, the position was an ideal fit for his talents. One day he was assigned to cover a ship's project in-country in Vietnam, involving a visit to an orphanage. He spent the day diligently observing the various humanitarian activities and taking notes, but came away unimpressed with the entire effort, for reasons that were never clear to me. He wrote an account of the day's activities that was rather poorly done and not nearly up to the standards that he had shown in prior efforts. I reviewed the story and gave him my frank opinion that it was unsatisfactory. I told him that if he ever wanted to be a good writer, he had to learn to write interesting accounts of events that did not necessarily appeal to him. Anyone, I told him, can write about a story that really excites him; but it is the really skilled writer who can turn a story that he finds ordinary into a piece of writing that the reader will find interesting, if not exciting.

A single lie destroys a whole reputation for integrity.
— *Baltasar Gracián y Morales*

The young Sailor took back the rejected draft and, several hours later, handed me a story that was a first-rate account of the ship's humanitarian trip to the orphanage. Not only was the story published in the ship's paper, where it received enthusiastic reviews, it was later sent to the type commander's staff, which in turn published the story in its newsletter.

Moral: Expect more from your folks. Challenge them to be better. They'll surprise you!

—*CAPT John Malone, USN*

CHAPTER 4

Salty Leadership Advice

While I recommend in the strongest terms to the respective officers, activity, vigilance, and firmness, I feel no less solicitude that their deportment may be marked with prudence, moderation, and good temper.

. . .

Always keep in mind that [your] countrymen are free men, and as such, are impatient of everything that bears the least mark of a domineering spirit . . . therefore, refrain, with the most guarded circumspection, from whatever has the semblance of haughtiness, rudeness, or insult.

. . .

Endeavor to overcome difficulties, if any are experienced, by a cool and temperate perseverance in . . . duty—by address and moderation, rather than by vehemence and violence.

—Alexander Hamilton, a 1791 letter
of advice to first officers of
Revenue-Marine Service,
precursor to the Coast Guard

In preparation for this book, we surveyed about 380 senior seagoing officers, representing some nine thousand years of experience. Many wrote in with comments and advice intended for the junior officer at sea.

This chapter provides a sample of those nuggets of advice from senior leaders. More are included in the Port watch, chapter 8. As you read them, take a moment to ponder the career of experience behind each of the writers and the words they choose to pass on to you, the next generation of seagoing leaders.

THE SLOWER YOU GO, THE SMALLER THE DENT

As a reserve lieutenant, I spent six weeks aboard the yard patrol boats at Annapolis participating in midshipmen summer cruises. A Merchant Marine captain led the program as reserve commander. He told me that "the slower you go the smaller the dent." Now that I am captain of a nonprofit medical aid vessel operating in the South Pacific, I remember that advice nearly every time I bring the ship alongside a pier.

> Miseries seem light to a soldier if the chief who imposes hardships on him also volunteers to share them.
>
> —Henri Francis, Comte de Ségur

But it also applies in other areas. Sometimes even when proceeding with deliberate caution, you still have to respond nearly instantly. For instance, you see the ship responding in an unanticipated direction and you have to rapidly determine what force is at your disposal to correct the situation: a mooring line, the rudder, more power or less, a tug, and so forth. And then you have to use that force appropriately. Going too slow can also be dangerous in some shiphandling scenarios.

But proceeding with deliberate caution is nearly always appropriate. You get an e-mail that makes you angry—do you blast right back with an emotionally charged attack leading to a relational shipwreck with a coworker, subordinate, or even boss? Or do you leave it in your inbox overnight and reply the next day with greater objectivity and rationality? Going slowly in your communications and relationships at every level reduces the dents you make on other people as you learn how to handle your own leaderSHIP responsibilities.

Take time to get to know and understand your people and to listen to them. It will make your maneuvering as a leader much more effective. As a third mate on a cargo ship, my captain had spent many years as a chief mate. He told me that the hardest part of his job was to let the chief mate do the job he was supposed to do. Now as a captain myself, I really understand that. Especially when you were good at a job you used to have and enjoyed it, it is tempting to jump in and try to do a job that is now assigned to someone else. That is a pretty fast way of undermining and demotivating your people. If you can do the job yourself, why do you need them? And if you don't need them, why are they there? People want to be in a place where they feel they are making a significant contribution. Besides that, if you spend too much time trying to do the jobs of other people, you will wear yourself out, eventually getting to the point where you don't even do your job well. You have to be willing to trust your people.

—*CAPT Jeremy Schierer, master of a nonprofit medical aid ship*

RESPONSIBILITY

I am always amazed at what you can get accomplished when there is a clear meeting of the minds between the supervisor and the worker. This is true whether it is the ship's captain giving a job directly to a junior officer, or the executive officer passing on task direction to a department head. One tenet I have always kept in mind is a famous quote from ADM Hyman Rickover, the founder of the Navy's nuclear power program. It should be well understood by new officers and our most senior officers alike. I've kept a copy of this succinct saying concerning responsibility posted in every stateroom I have occupied during nearly thirteen years afloat.

Rickover said:

> Responsibility is a unique concept, it can only reside in a single individual. You may share it with others, but your portion is not diminished. You may delegate it, but it is still with you. You may disclaim it, but you cannot divest yourself of it. Even if you do not recognize it or admit its presence, you cannot escape it. If responsibility is rightfully yours, no evasion or ignorance or passing the blame can shift the burden to someone else. Unless you can point your finger at the man who is responsible when something goes wrong, then you have never had anyone really responsible.
>
> —*RDML Steven Ratti, USCG*

The world belongs to the energetic.

—*Ralph Waldo Emerson*

JUNIOR OFFICERS AND SENIOR ENLISTED

Your most important asset is your senior enlisted teammates. It is imperative that the new officer show respect for these highly trained and experienced personnel from the first moment he or she steps on board. Enlisted personnel will initially respect the new officer due to rank. The new officer must immediately let them know that he respects them for their experience and loyalty. This mutual respect is critical to the bonding of the team and for optimum performance as a unit.

The chief petty officers (CPO) on the ship will ask the newly reporting officer's chief his impressions of the new officer. It is important that the new officer be seen as honest, interested, willing to learn and contribute, and having a good sense of what he knows and what he must still learn. If in doubt about "what he knows," the new officer should err on the side of "there's much I don't know." If the senior enlisted members of the crew see the new officer as a future leader they would be willing to serve with and follow, then they will take an interest in the new officer's professional development, sharing their years of experience and greatly reducing the learning curve. If they see the new officer as having a self-promoting agenda or as being a "know-it-all," the new officer will have a much more difficult time learning the necessary information required for being assigned and properly executing increased responsibilities.

I have not yet begun to fight!

—*John Paul Jones*

As my senior CPO said to me the first day I reported to my first ship, "Sir, I think we will get along just fine. You seem to be bright, enthusiastic, and interested. However, there are a couple of things I'd like you to remember: (1) Although you and I might not always agree, we will *never* disagree in front of the troops, and (2) in the event we still disagree on a matter in private and cannot resolve an issue between us, please consider that I have been in this Navy longer than you have been on the face of this Earth."

I still remember that conversation after almost thirty years . . . and I still appreciate my senior chief for grounding me in such a professional manner very early in my career.

—*LT Pete Parsons, USN*

A THREE-POINT LEADERSHIP MODEL

Point One: This point was my touchstone throughout my career. If every officer simply followed this model, we would have a solid leadership corps. It's from the writings of John Paul Jones, on the qualifications of a naval officer:

It is by no means enough that an officer of the Navy should be a capable mariner. He must be that, of course, but also a great deal more. He should be as well a gentleman of liberal education, refined manners, punctilious courtesy, and the nicest sense of personal honor. He should be the soul of tact, patience, justice, firmness, and charity. No meritorious act of a subordinate should escape his attention or be left to pass without its reward, even if the reward is only a word of approval. Conversely, he should not be blind to a single fault in any subordinate, though, at the same time, he should be quick and unfailing to distinguish error from malice, thoughtlessness from incompetency, and well-meant shortcoming from heedless or stupid blunder.

I cannot trust a man to control others
who cannot control himself.

—*Robert E. Lee*

Point Two: Leadership is the capacity to motivate others to achieve a mission, a goal, a task, or an objective. Good leadership is the capacity to motivate others to achieve in a fun environment. Great leadership is the capacity to motivate masses of people to achieve on a grand scale.

Point Three: I learned what I call the "golden rule" of leadership from one of my first skippers, who said, "Take a sincere interest in the people who work for you." My experience has validated this time and again; and if you simply do this one thing, you can make a myriad of mistakes and your people will take care of you. The interest has to be sincere, as subordinates will see right through insincerity.

—*CAPT Skip Lind, USN*

MINORITIES IN THE MILITARY

Minorities—they're your responsibility as well as the majority. They want to achieve, be recognized for good performance, and respected just like the others. Minorities have learned coping mechanisms in society that you may or may not understand, but listening is the best skill you can develop. Learn their story, celebrate their differences, and make them a voice on your team.

It ain't hard to be an officer, but it's damn hard to be a good officer.

—*Chief Petty Officer, USN*

I first encountered sexual harassment in boot camp. It was close to assault but luckily I was rescued by my new fellow shipmates. Imagine that being your sister or mother.

Take care of those who have a small voice and recognize it's twice as hard to succeed at the bottom if you have the additional burden (or gift, depending on your point of view) of being different in color, sex, religion, or sexual practice. Not everyone has the same opportunities growing up, so whether it's color or intellect, encourage the strengths and praise the successes.

The military creates great leaders; make not only your country proud but your Mom also. Leadership doesn't come from the insignia on your collar—it comes from the integrity of your character. Remember the golden rule: "Do unto others as you would have them do unto you." Treat everyone with respect and they will respect you.

—*Senior Chief Linda Blessing, USN*

THREE QUALITIES OF A LEADER

Leadership is not an abstract concept; it's the dynamic of accomplishing a mission through people. To me, the three most important traits are Integrity, Loyalty, and Enthusiasm.

Integrity involves truthfulness, of course, but also decisions made on principle, not expediency. Thus, people with integrity are fair and are predictable.

> The officer should wear his uniform as a judge his ermine, without a stain.
>
> —*Dahlgren*

Loyalty in a true leader is three-dimensional. It extends upward to the superiors who provide the tools with which we lead. It extends laterally to colleagues and contemporaries, and especially, it extends downward to those who look to us for guidance and career development.

Enthusiasm begets enthusiasm. When people observe enthusiasm, they conclude "This guy is going somewhere; I want to go with him." Men will follow you into hell, if they know you are for them. These qualities have worked effectively for decades.

—*RADM Matthias Backer, USN*

PERSONAL LEADERSHIP MOTTOS TO LIVE BY

Here are the mottos that I live by. Maybe they'll help you!

- Lead, follow, or get out of the way. Choose one.
- Act like you are in the best Navy in the world. To be the best requires high standards, so enforce the standards.
- Prior proper planning prevents poor performance.
- Find the instruction; read and follow it. Knowledge is power.
- Self-control—do not put yourself in a situation where you have to apologize. If you do, then humbly apologize and reconcile your differences.
- Character—the decision you make when no one is looking.

- It is ok to yell every once in a while, but if you abuse your voice, people will stop listening.
- Demonstrate intrusive leadership. Show your Sailor how to accomplish the task.
- Control your own destiny. If a problem arises, propose a solution. Soon everything will be done your way.
- Do not run away from problems. Turn them into learning opportunities.
- Give specific orders that cannot be misinterpreted.
- Take care of one another.
- Take out your frustration by improving the situation.
- Do not take your frustrations at work to your family at home.
- Get out of the Navy when you stop having fun.
- Bad news does not get better with age.
- "A failure to plan is a plan to fail."

—LCDR Gary Blumberg, USN

Men mean more than guns in the rating of a ship.

—John Paul Jones

FOUR PRINCIPLES

Four basic principles, taught me by others, might be useful for you too.

1. Work with the system. Know and respect laws, directives, policies, and practices, but recognize the differences between laws, directives, policies, and practices. You can count on change. Working with the system requires you to keep up to date with those changes. A chief petty officer at a four-star fleet staff taught me that lesson long ago. When contacting headquarters

with a request he regularly asked, "What are the rules today?"

2. The job is not done until the paperwork is finished. If you don't do paperwork well, learn. In spite of serious efforts and significant improvements to reduce paperwork, documentation remains essential. When you report to your seniors, brag about your staff and supporters. And just because you sent it, don't assume they got it. Keep copies. Check by phone or confirm by e-mail. Accept that you aren't the most important person in each overworked Sailor's life!

The difference between a good officer and a great one
is about ten seconds.

—*RADM Arleigh Burke*

---

3. Look sharp. Appearance gains credibility, respect, and influence. Those advantages benefit others, not just you. The level of your influence gives a viable voice for all those who work for you. Keep yourself in physical shape and attend to details of uniforms and grooming.

4. Develop friendships and social contacts. The military is more social than some of us are used to in civilian life. It often requires financial expense that we may not usually spend. Remember that money and time for memberships, dinners, and receptions are an investment, not just an expense. Spend it.

—*RADM Darold Bigger, USN, Chaplain Corps*

A CHIEF PETTY OFFICER ON LEADERSHIP

Leadership is a compilation of experience, work ethic, discipline, attitude, and character. As a chief petty officer with many years of experience dealing with young Sailors and young officers, one of my main goals was to always treat everyone as fairly and equally as I could. I wanted everyone to know that he or she is a valuable resource within the division or the squadron. By setting the example of what leadership is, everyone knows who and what you are and that there are no shortcuts in achieving success.

A strong work ethic not only keeps young minds strong and viable, but it instills in every Sailor a promise that for hard work, good things will happen. Whether it's studying for the next higher pay grade or accomplishing a successful underway replenishment, a job well done reaps many rewards personally and professionally. A strong discipline, tempered with a good attitude about self and those around you, will lead to your ability to sustain mission accomplishments that bring honor and pride not only to yourself, but those who serve under you.

A Man of War is the best Ambassador.

—*Oliver Cromwell*

Finally character is of the utmost importance, for if you want to be an effective leader, you must always set the example if you want young Sailors to follow. Leading by example exemplifies a strong character; it sets the tone for how you will succeed, not only in the Navy but also in civilian life and the world. Lack of strong character, or weakness in morals and civility, will make your subordinates question your ability to lead. Once that occurs, your trustworthiness will be compromised, and you will never regain their confidence again. Always be above reproach in your morals and convictions, and never sacrifice them for the sake of expedience or false friendships.

—*CPO Delbert Mitchell, USN*

CHAPTER 5

What Seniors Say: The Newest Leadership List

It is by no means enough that an officer of the Navy be a capable mariner. He must be that, of course, but also a great deal more. He should be as well a gentleman of liberal education, refined manners, punctilious courtesy, and the nicest sense of personal honor.

He should be the soul of tact, patience, justice, firmness, and charity. No meritorious act of a subordinate should escape his attention or be left to pass without its reward, even if the reward is only a word of approval. Conversely, he should not be blind to a single fault in any subordinate, though at the same time, he should be quick and unfailing to distinguish error from malice, thoughtfulness from incompetency, and well-meant shortcoming from heedless or stupid blunder.

In one word, every commander should keep constantly before him the great truth, that to be well obeyed, he must be perfectly esteemed.

—John Paul Jones

In chapter 2 we provided a few of the leadership lists resident in thirty-five of the thousands of books written on leadership. When we looked at those lists, we saw some threads that were repeated again and again. And you'll notice that these lists include:

- what a leader should be (traits)
- what a leader should be capable of (skills, or competencies)

Why another leadership list?

All the lists above are valuable. Many of them are germane to the young seagoing officer. Many of them are prepared by authors and editors with years of salty experience. However, all of them reflected the bias and experience of the respective authors. Each was individualized based on its source. My goal was to create a list based simply on a survey of senior seagoing officers. Any one young officer could ask a more senior officer, "What traits do you think I need to be a leader?" My goal was ask that question several hundred times and aggregate the cumulative results.

The expected outcome: the cumulative wisdom of nine thousand years of seagoing experience, all in a single list of the primary traits desired in a seagoing junior officer.

THE QUESTION: WHAT WE ASKED, AND HOW

We established a website with a survey engine. We invited members of the sea services (Navy, Coast Guard, and Merchant Marine) to visit the website and to participate. We solicited inputs by e-mailing to senior officers in all services and to senior staff at the maritime academies.

> An officer is set apart, clothed differently, and given distinguishing marks. His greater responsibilities are rewarded with greater privileges. There is some insistence on a show of respect. He is removed from that intimate contact with the men under his command which can throw such a strain upon the relationship of subordinates.
>
> —GEN Sir John W. Hackett

The respondents were asked to choose "the primary traits required of the successful junior officer at sea" from the seventy-six potential traits listed in this table.

Seventy-Six Potential Positive Traits in a Junior Officer at Sea		
Ability to Build Teams	Foresight	Positive Attitude
Accountability	Imagination	Professionalism
Adaptability	Initiative	Prudence
Agreeableness	Innovation, Creativity	Resourcefulness
Ambition	Inquisitiveness	Responsiveness
Analytical Thinking	Insight	Scholarship
Attention to Detail	Inspiration	Self-Control
Boldness and Daring	Instinct	Selflessness
Caution	Integrity, Honor	Sense of Humor
Character, Strength of	Intellect	Sensitivity
Commitment	Interpersonal Sensitivity	Sociability
Conscience	Intuition	Speaking Ability
Conscientiousness	Judgment	Spirituality
Conviction	Leadership Presence	Tactical Proficiency
Decisiveness	Loyalty	Teamwork
Dedication	Maturity	Technical Competence
Dependability	Military Bearing	Tenacity
Determination	Moral Courage	Tidiness
Diligence	Optimism	Trustworthiness
Discipline	Passion	Versatility
Drive	Patience	Vigor
Emotional Intelligence	Perseverance	Vision
Empathy	Physical Courage	Work Ethic
Endurance	Physical Fitness	Writing Ability
Enthusiasm	Politeness	
Focus	Political Awareness	

THE RESPONDENTS

Approximately 380 people responded to the survey. They represented, cumulatively, nearly nine thousand years of experience, or an average of about twenty-four years per respondent. Of those that responded, 58 percent characterized their service as "active," while 42 percent considered themselves "retired." Most (93 percent) were male, and 7 percent were female.

The following table indicates the breakout by service:

	Response	
Answer Options	(%)	(Count)
Navy	74.3	284
Marine Corps	2.4	9
Coast Guard	4.2	16
Merchant Marine	6.5	25
Other	12.6	48

The following table indicates the breakout by seniority for those in uniform. For simplicity and clarity, only Navy and Coast Guard ranks are shown.

	Response	
Answer Options	(%)	(Count)
E-7 (Chief Petty Officer)	6.6	25
E-8 (Senior Chief Petty Officer)	2.7	10
E-9 (Master Chief Petty Officer)	3.4	13
WO (Warrant Officer)	0.8	3
O-1 (Ensign)	0.8	3
O-2 (Lieutenant Junior Grade)	2.1	8
O-3 (Lieutenant)	6.9	26
O-4 (Lieutenant Commander)	12.5	47
O-5 (Commander)	22.0	83
O-6 (Captain)	28.1	106
O-7 (Rear Admiral [lower half])	6.1	23
O-8 (Rear Admiral [upper half])	4.2	16
O-9 (Vice Admiral)	0.8	3

Of those in the Merchant Marine, the following indicates their seniority:

	Response	
Answer Options	(%)	(Count)
3rd mate or 3rd asst eng	2.9	11
2nd mate or 2nd asst eng	2.1	8
1st mate or 1st asst eng	1.6	6
master or chief engineer	10.5	40

I have yet to find the man, however exalted his station,
who did not do better work and put forth greater effort under
a spirit of approval than under a spirit of criticism.

—*Charles Schwab, industrialist*

THE RESULTS

Each respondent was allowed up to eight "primary" traits, and eight "secondary" traits. These votes were weighted, with primary being scored with twice the weight of a secondary, to form a total score for each trait.

The top ten most-selected traits are listed below.

Top Ten Desired Traits	Score	Top Ten Desired Traits	Score
Integrity and Honor	465	Work Ethic	311
Character, Strength of	354	Dependability	310
Trustworthiness	317	Initiative	302
Judgment	316	Positive Attitude	290
Accountability	314	Attention to Detail	253

The least-selected traits, with the lowest scores, are listed below.

Least Selected Traits	Score	Least Selected Traits	Score
Sensitivity	7	Spirituality	14
Scholarship	7	Prudence	17
Tidiness	8	Vigor	18
Political Awareness	11	Agreeableness	19
Politeness	12	Insight	23

Every danger of a military character to which the United States is
exposed can be met best outside her own territory—at sea.

—*RADM Alfred Thayer Mahan*

Finally the following table shows all seventy-six traits, ranked in order of total score:

All Traits, Ranked by Total Score		
1 Integrity, Honor	27 Tactical Proficiency	53 Inquisitiveness
2 Character, Strength of	28 Selflessness	54 Boldness and Daring
3 Trustworthiness	29 Self-Control	55 Optimism
4 Judgment	30 Speaking Ability	56 Vision
5 Accountability	31 Intellect	57 Conscience
6 Work Ethic	32 Military Bearing	58 Conviction
7 Dependability	33 Writing Ability	59 Empathy
8 Initiative	34 Maturity	60 Ambition
9 Positive Attitude	35 Dedication	61 Physical Courage
10 Professionalism	36 Conscientiousness	62 Sociability
11 Attention to Detail	37 Emotional Intelligence	63 Intuition
12 Adaptability	38 Innovation and Creativity	64 Inspiration
13 Decisiveness	39 Foresight	65 Interpersonal Sensitivity
14 Resourcefulness	40 Determination	66 Caution
15 Moral Courage	41 Physical Fitness	67 Insight
16 Teamwork	42 Patience	68 Agreeableness
17 Leadership Presence	43 Tenacity	69 Vigor
18 Commitment	44 Drive	70 Prudence
19 Analytical Thinking	45 Focus	71 Spirituality
20 Ability to Build Teams	46 Responsiveness	72 Politeness
21 Technical Competence	47 Versatility	73 Political Awareness
22 Sense of Humor	48 Diligence	74 Tidiness
23 Enthusiasm	49 Instinct	75 Scholarship
24 Discipline	50 Passion	76 Sensitivity
25 Perseverance	51 Endurance	
26 Loyalty	52 Imagination	

Now, the above lists are very interesting, and they do provide some useful results. But the review of individual words, in a list of seventy-six traits, might lead to some erroneous conclusions.

Marines have a reasonable expectation that their leaders will come up with plans that will accomplish the mission and give them the best possible chance of succeeding. They do not ask for certainty, just the best possible preparation and skills from their leaders.

—USMC Field Manuel 1-0, Leading Marines

What if we grouped the seventy-six traits into a smaller set of more general categories?

Many of the seventy-six traits are related—they refer to a common, more general attribute. For instance "integrity" and "character" are very similar and could be grouped. When we analyzed the seventy-six traits, they seemed to form into seven larger areas, as shown on the chart.

Traits Grouped into Seven Areas

WORK ETHIC & INITIATIVE	CHARACTER & INTEGRITY	TEAMING & LEADERSHIP
Ambition	Accountability	Ability to Build Teams
Boldness and Daring	Character, Strength of	Inspiration
Caution	Conscience	Leadership Presence
Commitment	Conscientiousness	Loyalty
Decisiveness	Conviction	Professionalism
Dedication	Dependability	Selfishness
Determination	Discipline	Teamwork
Diligence	Integrity and Honor	**SKILLS**
Drive	Moral Courage	Attention to Detail
Endurance	Physical Courage	Military Bearing
Enthusiasm	Self-Control	Patience
Focus	Trustworthiness	Physical Fitness
Imagination	**PERSONALITY**	Politeness
Initiative	Adaptability	Speaking Ability
Passion	Agreeableness	Tactical Proficiency
Perseverance	Emotional Intelligence	Technical Competence
Positive Attitude	Empathy	Tidiness
Prudence	Interpersonal Sensitivity	Writing Ability
Resourcefulness	Optimism	**JUDGMENT & MATURITY**
Responsiveness	Political Awareness	Foresight
Tenacity	Sense of Humor	Insight
Versatility	Sensitivity	Instinct
Vigor	Sociability	Intuition
Work Ethic	Spirituality	Judgment
INTELLECT		Maturity
Analytical Thinking		Vision
Innovation and Creativity		
Inquisitiveness		
Intellect		
Scholarship		

It's interesting to see how the 380 senior seagoing leaders emphasized these seven potential trait groups. To organize by trait groups, we analyzed and normalized the responses across those groups to account for the varying number of traits in each group.

The following table shows the emphasis these collective leaders placed on those seven larger areas:

Scores by Trait Group	(%)
Character and Integrity	203
Teaming	155
Work Ethic and Initiative	109
Skills	99
Judgment and Maturity	92
Intellect	83
Personality	62

As you can see, they emphasized character and integrity issues above all else. Next, they wanted a professional teammate—a good shipmate. Third, they valued initiative and a strong work ethic.

What does all this mean?

The bottom-line results are clear and perhaps self-evident.

We queried 380 seagoing leaders representing nine thousand years of experience. They placed six thousand votes against a tally of seventy-six different potential traits they wanted to see in a junior officer assigned to their ship.

And what did they want? Character and Integrity (Honesty). A good shipmate who can work as part of a larger team (Teammate). A hard worker with good attitude and the initiative to get things done (Hard-Working).

They wanted an Honest, Hard-Working Teammate.

They felt that skills could be taught and that judgment and maturity weren't as important, because they would come in time. They felt that personality wasn't as important. (But before you assume that an unpleasant shipboard personality is acceptable, remember that there is a healthy dose of "personality" embedded in the ability to work well on teams, which was highly valued.)

So there it is—the results of the survey—the bottom line of the latest leadership list: To be a successful junior officer at sea, these collective old salts say, be an

Honest, Hard-Working Teammate.

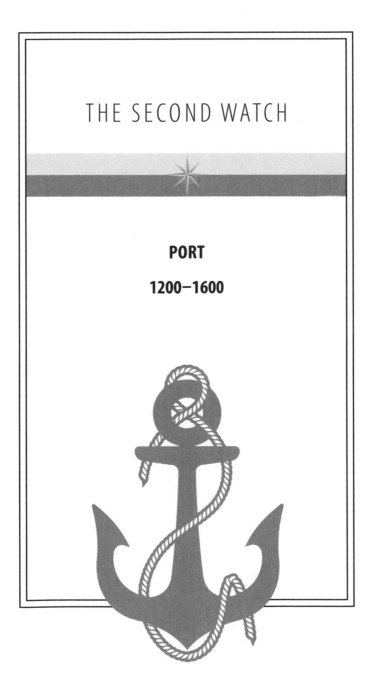

THE SECOND WATCH

PORT

1200–1600

CHAPTER 6

MORE LEADERSHIP LISTS

Sea power in the broad sense . . . includes not
only the military strength afloat, that rules the
sea or any part of it by force of arms, but also the
peaceful commerce and shipping from which
alone a military fleet naturally and healthfully
springs, and on which it securely rests.

—REAR ADMIRAL ALFRED THAYER MAHAN

ADVICE, RECOMMENDATIONS, PRINCIPLES, AND RULES

Remember that back in chapter 2, on the previous
watch, we discussed that leadership is prone to lists.
Back then, we reviewed lists of traits and of skills.
This chapter looks at three additional buckets of lists: Advice,
Models, and Codes.

Remember, leadership is about traits—about what you
are. It's about skill sets and competencies—what you *do*. But
it's also about principles and sets of rules, which often stray
over into desired attributes and competencies. Each of the ten
lists in this section will provide advice, or recommendations,
or rules, which have been pulled from the previously mentioned thirty-five books and ten thousand pages.

Again, we'll look at seagoing texts, and those from other
services, and then those from business and academia.

The Division Officers Guide provides a wonderful and
straightforward list, called "Principles of Naval Leadership."

- Know your job
- Know yourself
- Know and take care of your subordinates
- Set a positive example
- Project a clear vision and communicate effectively
- Direct, motivate, and develop subordinates
- Demonstrate effective management skills
- Build effective teams

That's a great, classic list. Any young officer should post that list above his or her desk.

Each year, the Navy's Center for Personal and Professional Development publishes the Navy Leader Planning Guide, which contains calendars, references, historic information, checklists, phone numbers, and other data vital to young leaders at sea. The Navy will give you a copy, free.

Among many other interesting lists, it provides the "11 Principles of Naval Leadership":

1. Know yourself and seek self improvement.
2. Be technically and tactically proficient.
3. Know your subordinates and look out for their welfare.
4. Keep your subordinates informed.
5. Set the example.
6. Ensure the task is understood, supervised, and accomplished.
7. Train your unit as a team.
8. Make sound and timely decisions.
9. Develop a sense of responsibility among your subordinates.
10. Employ your command in accordance with its capabilities.

11. Seek responsibility and take responsibility for your actions.

For nearly 110 years, *The Blue Jacket's Manual* has guided Sailors with advice and wisdom. The centennial edition of this classic, written by LCDR Thomas Cutler, USN (Ret.), offers the following ten leadership principles or practices:

1. Reverse Roles (consider the Golden Rule)
2. Take Responsibility
3. Set the Example
4. Praise in Public; Correct in Private
5. Be Consistent, but Not Inflexible
6. Know Your Job
7. Do Not Micromanage
8. Practice Good Followership
9. Don't Be One of the Gang
10. Keep Your Subordinates Informed

One of the most valuable qualities of a commander is a flair for putting himself in the right place at the vital time.

—*Field Marshal Sir William Slim*

Michael Abrashoff was commanding officer of the guided-missile destroyer USS *Benfold* (DDG-65). After his successful tour as CO, he wrote the book *It's Your Ship*, which is now used as a leadership text at some maritime academies. He provides eleven major pieces of advice, each of which has subcomponents as indicated:

1. Take Command
2. Lead by Example
   – It's funny how often the problem is you.

- Never forget your effect on people.
- Leaders know how to be accountable.
- Never fail the *Washington Post* test[1].
- Obey even when you disagree.

3. Listen Aggressively
- See the ship through the crew's eyes.
- Find round people for round holes.
- Use the power of "word magic."

4. Communicate Purpose and Meaning
- Make your crew think: "we can do anything."
- Open up the clogged channels.
- After creating a great brand, defend it.
- Freedom creates discipline.

5. Create a Climate of Trust
- Even the worst screwup may be redeemable.
- Welcome the bad-news messenger.
- Protect your people from lunatic bosses.
- Being the best carries responsibility.

6. Look for Results, Not Salutes
- Help knock down the barriers.
- Let your crew feel free to speak up.
- Free your crew from "top-down-it is."
- Nurture the freedom to fail.
- Innovation knows no rank.
- Challenge your crew beyond its reach.

7. Take Calculated Risks
- Bet on the people who think for themselves.
- Take a chance on a promising sailor.
- If a rule doesn't make sense, break it.
- If a rule does make sense, break it carefully.

8. Go Beyond Standard Procedure
- Keep your priorities in focus.

---

[1] This is a common test of an ethical decision: "If I had to read about this decision on the front page of the *Washington Post* tomorrow, would I be okay with it?"

- Stay ahead of the competition.
- Push the envelope for innovation.
- Volunteering benefits everyone.
- Go for the obvious. It's probably a winner.
- Don't work harder. Work smarter.
- Don't fight stupidity. Use it.

9. Build Up Your People
   - Little things make big successes.
   - Trust people. They usually prove you're right.
   - Newbies are important. Treat them well.
   - Be the rising tide that lifts all boats.
   - Build up your bosses.
   - Expect the best from your crew. You will get it.
   - Build a strong, deep bench.
   - Counsel continuously—and honestly.

10. Generate Unity
    - Forget diversity. Train for unity.
    - Deal out punishment strictly but fairly.

11. Improve Your People's Quality of Life
    - Fun with your friends makes a happy ship.
    - The first priority: good food.
    - In heavy times, lighten up.
    - Let the crew show off the ship.
    - The secret of good work? Good play.

The buck stops here.

—*Harry Truman*

As Commander Abrashoff learned leadership lessons while serving as a leader, so too did MAJ John Chapman, U.S. Army. He wrote up his lessons-learned in the book *Muddy Boots Leadership.* He concludes with his "Ten Rules to Live By for Leaders":

1. Be at the critical time and place—every day has (at least) one.
2. Everything in life is a graded event.
3. Common sense counts.
4. Discipline begins with self-discipline.
5. Wear your heart on your sleeve; your soldiers must know how you feel.
6. Subordinates learn by your example, whether you intend it or not.
7. Five minutes' checking on the guards in a freezing rain at midnight is worth a year of payday speeches.
8. Considering input doesn't make you weak; it makes you smart.
9. You gain authority by giving it.
10. What you see is as important as what you choose not to see.

In a similar way, but in a more institutional sense, the Marine Corps has memorialized its view of proper leadership in *Field Manual 1-0, Leading Marines*. It lists eleven steps to become a leader of Marines:

1. Be technically and tactically proficient.
2. Know yourself and seek self-improvement.
3. Know your Marines and look out for their welfare.
4. Keep your Marines informed.
5. Set the example.
6. Ensure the task is understood, supervised, and accomplished.
7. Train your Marines as a team.
8. Make sound and timely decisions.
9. Develop a sense of responsibility among your subordinates.
10. Employ your unit in accordance with its capabilities.

11. Seek responsibility, and take responsibility for your actions.

Speaking of Marine Corps leadership, two former Marines left the military, went into the business world, and later wrote *Semper Fi: Business Leadership the Marine Corps Way*. In the book's section "Leading the Rank and File," they described eighteen leadership commandments to achieve excellence:

1. Create a culture that exalts the workforce.
2. Inspire through personal example.
3. Understand that the employee who feels cared for will care about the company.
4. Combine fire-breathing enthusiasm with solicitous mentoring.
5. Empower those closest to the task to make decisions.
6. Expand departmental pride into a corporate-wide phenomenon.
7. Institutionalize the supervisor as the corporate teacher.
8. Recognize followership as the precursor to leadership.
9. Convert personal ambition into commitment to the corporate mission.
10. Implement a "manager's school" for all levels of management.
11. Require and support continuing education.
12. Empower and delegate, but be available to your subordinates.
13. Expect all associates to keep pace with the strides of the organization.
14. Implement company-wide "subject readiness" tests.
15. Promote constructive competition.

16. Provide all associates with a communications path all the way to the top.
17. Reach out to the families of the workforce and managerial staff.
18. Exalt seniority, while maintaining performance expectations.

Curse ruthless time! Curse our mortality! How cruelly short is the allotted span for all we must cram into it!

—*Winston S. Churchill*

Dale Carnegie was the businessman who wrote the classic *How to Win Friends and Influence People.* (If you haven't read it, get it today!) His company, Dale Carnegie Training, wrote the book *Leadership Mastery: How to Challenge Yourself and Others to Greatness.* It provides advice in the form of a list of "practical tactics and techniques":

1. Master the Decision-Making Process.
2. Clearly Articulate Expectations.
3. Only Make Promises That You Can Keep.
4. Use Humor Whenever Possible.
5. Be Respected and Liked.
6. Master One-on-One Communication.
7. Be Consistent.
8. Understand the Four Stages of Competency.[2]
9. Always Respond Within 24 Hours.

---

[2] The first stage is unconscious incompetence: you're no good, and you don't know it. The second stage is conscious incompetence: you're still no good, but at least you recognize that fact. The third stage is conscious competence: you're good, you're skilled, but you have to think about it to be that way. The fourth and highest stage is unconscious competence: you're really good and don't have to think about it—it becomes natural.

In a similar practical vein, *Leadership for Dummies* listed "The Axioms of Leadership." It provides a useful set of rules for any young leader to follow:

1. Provide a check and balance on managers.
2. Use common sense.
3. Hang your goals on the wall.
4. Make a contract with your team.
5. Keep the task simple and obvious.
6. Change your criteria for picking managers.
7. Focus on people, not systems.
8. Take the long view.
9. Break goals down to a manageable size.
10. Never miss an opportunity to rethink.
11. Renovate before you innovate.
12. Focus on vision and goals.

Luck is the residue of design.

—*Branch Rickey*

A far more nuanced view of the complexities of leadership is provided in *The Contrarian's Guide to Leadership*, by Stephen Sample. The author uses his book to teach a set of nine lessons for the leader who is maturing beyond basic leadership skills:

1. Think "gray." Become comfortable in the gray area between black and white. Don't get carried away categorizing things as good or bad, true or false, friend or foe.
2. Listen artfully. Use listening to acquire new ideas and gather new information.

3. Experts can be saviors, and they can be charlatans. Be careful, and be able to distinguish what kind of expert you're dealing with.
4. You are what you read. Read the right things!
5. Two rules on decisions. First, never make a decision yourself that can reasonably be delegated to a subordinate. Second, never make a decision today that can reasonably be put off to tomorrow.
6. Know which hill you're willing to die on.
7. Work for those who work for you.
8. Follow the leader. Leaders create followers.
9. Don't just be the leader; do the leader. Do the hard things you must do to fulfill the role of leader. Leadership isn't a state of "being"—it is a state of "doing."

Peter Drucker is the grandfather of management and leadership study. His classic book is entitled *The Effective Executive: The Definitive Guide to Getting the Right Things Done.* In it he identifies eight practices of successful executives. This is a formidable list—in eight short practices, it encapsulates the essence of the effective leader.

1. They asked: "What needs to be done?"
2. They asked: "What is right for the enterprise?"
3. They developed action plans.
4. They took responsibility for decisions.
5. They took responsibility for communications.
6. They were focused on opportunities rather than problems.
7. They ran productive meetings.
8. They thought and said "we" rather than "I."

Not as time proven as Drucker, but nonetheless useful, is another list contained in *Leadership for Dummies*. It defines the six key responsibilities of a leader:

1. Developing a Vision
2. Coming Up with a Plan
3. Working toward Goals
4. Building a Strong Team
5. Figuring out What Your Team Needs, and Giving It to Them
6. Getting People to Follow through with Their Responsibilities

———————⚓———————

Finally, just as we saw Churchill's views on competencies, we can refer to *Churchill on Leadership* to get some advice and about a dozen "rules" from that great leader.

His guidelines on personnel and administration:

- Establish trust in your subordinates.
- Give clear direction.
- Back up your people through thick and thin.
- Keep fully informed; get your information directly from the source.
- Stick to priorities.
- Have a consistent method and discipline.

His thought process for leaders:

- Always concentrate on the broad view and the central features of the problem at hand.
- Factor in risk and chance by keeping things in proper proportion.
- Keep open to changing your mind in the presence of new facts.
- Be careful not to look too far ahead.

- Avoid excessive perfectionism.
- Don't make decisions for decision's sake.

I do believe in the spiritual nature of human beings.
To some it's a strange or outdated idea, but I believe there is such
a thing as a human spirit. There is a spiritual dimension
to man which should be nurtured.

—*Aung San Suu Kyi*

Leadership traits and attributes. Leadership skill sets and competencies. Leadership principles and sets of rules. How much more can you take? Just one more bucket of leadership lists: leadership models, or constructs.

MODELS

As we said before, leadership is about being—traits and attributes. It's about doing—skill sets and competencies. It's about sets of rules to provide guidance and govern behavior. All those nuances and views are contained in the different models one uses to describe leadership, and the development of leaders.

Let's look at the different leadership models hidden within those ten thousand pages, and let's start with two very useful models from the Coast Guard.

The commandant of the Coast Guard issued Commandant Instruction M5351.3 in May 2006. The purpose of this instruction is to establish a single, uniform leadership development framework for the entire Coast Guard. It is constructed around the Coast Guard's twenty-eight leadership competencies, which are organized into four primary groups. Notice how each group builds upon its predecessor;

the leader starts with leading self, then leading others, then leading organizations.

- Leading Self
- Accountability and Responsibility
- Followership
- Self-Awareness and Learning
- Aligning Values
- Health and Well-Being
- Personal Conduct
- Technical Proficiency

Anyone can dabble, but once you've made that commitment, your blood has that particular thing in it, and it's very hard for people to stop you.

—Bill Cosby

Leading Others
- Effective Communications
- Influencing Others
- Respect for Others and Diversity Management
- Team Building
- Taking Care of People
- Mentoring

Leading Performance and Change
- Customer Focus
- Management and Process Improvement
- Decision Making and Problem Solving
- Conflict Management
- Creativity and Innovation
- Vision Development and Implementation

Leading the Coast Guard
- Stewardship
- Technology Management
- Financial Management

- Human Resource Management
- Partnering
- External Awareness
- Entrepreneurship
- Political Savvy
- Strategic Thinking

⚓

Another leadership model is provided in *Character in Action: The Coast Guard on Leadership*. In it, authors Donald Phillips and ADM James Loy lay out an excellent plan for developing as a leader.

Step One: Set the Foundation
- Define the Culture and Live the Values
- Select the Best
- Promote Team Over Self
- Instill a Commitment to Excellence

Step Two: Focus on People
- Eliminate the Frozen Middle (middle management opposed to change)
- Cultivate Caring Relationships
- Build Strong Alliances
- Create an Effective Communication System

Progress always involves risks. You can't steal second base and keep your foot on first.

—*Frederick B. Wilcox*

Step Three: Instill a Bias for Action
- Make Change the Norm
- Encourage Decisiveness
- Empower the Young
- Give Priority to Those in the Field

Step Four: Ensure the Future
- Leverage Resources
- Sponsor Continual Learning
- Spotlight Excellence
- Honor History and Tradition

⚓

VADM James Stockdale provides an entirely different model for leadership in *Ethics and the Military Profession: Moral Foundations of Leadership.* In that book, COL Paul Rousch, USMC, writes about Stockdale's model for "Value- and Principle-Centered Leadership." As you'll recall, Stockdale was awarded the Medal of Honor as a POW in Vietnam, was later president of the Naval War College and the Citadel, and was Ross Perot's vice presidential running mate.

The Stockdale Leadership Model: Value- and Principle Centered Leadership:

Leaders are imbued with national and professional values.
- Their reference points are the Constitution and their services' core values.
- They incorporate these values into five leadership roles: Moralist, Teacher, Jurist, Steward, and Philosopher.

Leaders in the role of *moralist* make plain the good by the way they live their lives.
- Leaders are people of honor.
- Leaders demonstrate a disciplined lifestyle for emulation by their followers.
- Leaders exercise a priority of loyalties.

Leaders in the role of *jurist* make decisions, rules, and policies based on the strength of their character.

– Leaders hold themselves accountable for all their units do or fail to do.

– Leaders enhance their followers' ability to know what is right and do what is right.

– Leaders act upon well-placed conviction.

Leaders in the role of *teacher* provide a sense of perspective and set the moral, social, and particularly the motivational climate in a unit.

– Leaders appeal to their followers' highest aspirations.

– Leaders create confidence in their followers by serving as the catalyst for decisive, forceful action when appropriate.

– Leaders create a climate which promotes unit cohesion.

– Leaders enhance unit effectiveness.

Leaders in the role of *steward* invest their lives in the lives of their followers.

– Leaders view themselves as servants.

– Leaders guard the fundamental dignity of their followers.

– Leaders understand human nature and value individual differences.

Leaders in the role of *philosopher* persevere "when virtue is not rewarded and evil is not punished."

– Leaders do their duty because it is their duty.

– Leaders know how to deal with uncertainty and adapt to change.

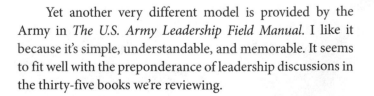

Yet another very different model is provided by the Army in *The U.S. Army Leadership Field Manual.* I like it because it's simple, understandable, and memorable. It seems to fit well with the preponderance of leadership discussions in the thirty-five books we're reviewing.

The model is *be, know, do.*

Be consists of Values and Attributes.
- Values include Loyalty, Duty, Respect, Selfless Service, Honor, Integrity, and Courage.
- Attributes include Mental, Physical, and Emotional traits.

Know consists of Skills: Interpersonal, Conceptual, Technical, and Tactical.

Do consists of Influencing, Operating, and Improving.
- Influencing means Communicating, Decision Making, and Motivating.
- Operating means Planning, Preparing, Executing, and Assessing.
- Improving means Developing, Building, and Learning.

Since shortly after 9/11, the Coast Guard has been a component within the Department of Homeland Security (DHS). Within the Coast Guard's official *Instruction on Leadership*, it lists the DHS five-step model for leadership competence. Like the Coast Guard model shown previously, it builds step by step, with each step requiring competence in its predecessor first. This model is broad enough to make sense in virtually all organizations, both military and civilian.

Core Competencies (all employees, including junior newcomers)
- Communication
- Influencing/Negotiating
- Customer Service
- Resilience
- Interpersonal Skills
- Continual Learning

- Flexibility
- Integrity/Honesty

Team or Project Leader
- Team Building
- Technical Credibility
- Problem Solving
- Accountability
- Decisiveness

Supervisor
- Human Resource Management
- Leveraging Diversity
- Conflict Management
- Service Motivation

Manager
- Technology Management
- Financial Management
- Creativity and Innovation
- Partners

The leader has something which the others want and which only he can provide . . . a capacity to help people in the overcoming of the difficulty which faces them in a joint enterprise.

—*Sir John Hackett*

Executive
- External Awareness
- Vision
- Strategic Thinking
- Entrepreneurship
- Political Savvy

⚓

One final model is provided in the business book *The Leadership Challenge: How to Keep Getting Extraordinary*

Things Done in Organizations. The authors suggest five fundamental practices of exemplary leadership, each of which has two primary commitments.

Practice 1: Challenge the Process. Leaders venture out. They are pioneers.
  – Commitment: Search out challenging opportunities to change, grow, innovate, and improve.
  – Commitment: Experiment, take risks, and learn from the accompanying mistakes.

Practice 2: Inspire a Shared Vision. Leaders breathe life into the hopes and dreams of others and enable them to see the exciting possibilities that the future holds.
  – Commitment: Envision an uplifting and ennobling future.
  – Commitment: Enlist others in a common vision by appealing to their values, interests, hopes, and dreams.

Practice 3: Enable Others to Act. Leaders enlist the support and assistance of all those who must make the project work. They enable others, through trust.
  – Commitment: Foster collaboration by promoting cooperative goals and building trust.
  – Commitment: Strengthen people by giving power away, providing choice, developing competence, assigning critical tasks, and offering visible support.

Practice 4: Model the Way. Leaders model through personal example and dedicated execution.
  – Commitment: Set the example by behaving in ways that are consistent with shared values.
  – Commitment: Achieve small wins that promote consistent progress and build commitment.

Practice 5: Encourage the Heart. Leaders encourage the hearts of their constituents to carry on.

    – Commitment: Recognize individual contributions to the success of every project.

    – Commitment: Celebrate team accomplishments regularly.

> Far better is it to dare mighty things, to win glorious triumphs, even though checkered by failure . . . than to rank with those poor spirits who neither enjoy nor suffer much, because they live in a gray twilight that knows not victory nor defeat.
>
> —*Theodore Roosevelt*

Before we end this chapter on leadership lists, let's look at the codes associated with service as an officer.

CODES

As we close this list of lists, let us refer to what is often the shortest lists—the codes of conduct. They are often encapsulated in a few words, which can form a code. The word "code," in this context, means a system of principles or rules. It comes from the Latin word meaning the trunk of a tree, because codes were originally written on wooden tablets.

The Navy's Core Values: Honor, Courage, and Commitment

The Coast Guard's Core Values: Honor, Respect, Devotion to Duty

A Code for Naval Leaders (originally from the Navy Policy Book):

Leadership is the essence of our profession.
People are the Navy's most valuable asset.
Provide recognition to deserving people.
Listen to your people.
Accept change and plan for uncertainty.

The West Point Motto: Duty, Honor, Country

The Core Values of Maine Maritime Academy's Regiment of Midshipmen: Honor, Loyalty, Devotion to Duty

> The Captain carried them all. For him, there was no fixed watch, no time set aside when he was free to relax and, if he could, to sleep. He was strong, calm, uncomplaining, and wonderfully dependable. That was the sort of captain to have.
>
> —*Nicholas Monsarratt,* The Cruel Sea

The Armed Forces Officer lists the following code concerning the character of an officer:

Honor: the compelling moral motivation to do the right thing at the right time.

Respect: The positive regard one person evidences for the shared humanity of another.

Duty: A moral obligation to place accomplishment of the assigned task before all personal needs and apprehensions.

Service: The officer is the servant of the nation. Service entails dedicating one's very life to something higher and more important than one's own gratification.

Excellence: A deep-seated personal passion for continuous improvement, innovation, and exemplary results in all endeavors.

Courage: The will to act rightly in the face of physical, personal or professional danger, or adversity.

Commitment: Total dedication to success.

Loyalty: A true, willing, and unfailing devotion to a cause.

Integrity: The willingness to do what is right even when no one is looking. The moral compass.

I find the great thing in this world is not so much where we stand, as in what direction we are moving. To reach [a point] we must sail sometimes with the wind and sometimes against it, but we must sail, and not drift, nor lie at anchor.

—*Oliver Wendell Holmes*

LESSONS TO DRAW FROM THE LISTS

What lessons can we draw from all this? Between chapters 2 and 6, we just skipped over the wavetops of thirty-five books written by dozens of authors, comprising some ten thousand pages of leadership advice. What does it all mean?

It means that leadership can be described in many different ways. That there is no one leadership way, and there is no one way to describe leadership. But we can still draw lessons from the lists. For instance, if we analyze the lists themselves, the following twenty-seven leadership words appear most frequently:

Twenty-Seven Leadership Words		
know	moral	physical
make	skills	commitment
self	responsibility	development
people	focus	honor
service	vision	followers
team	create	example
effective	press	decisions
courage	build	trust
others	lessons	plan

Courage. Responsibility. Vision. Commitment. Service. Notice how those words recur in many of the books on leadership.

And, if you look closely at the lists, you'll see common themes:

- Knowing your job
- Taking care of your people
- Delegation and follow-up
- Loyalty to the team and the cause
- Being an honorable person of character
- Setting goals and helping others achieve

In other words, while a thousand people will paint their picture of leadership in a thousand different ways, they'll use only a dozen or so brushstrokes and just a few colors. There are commonalities.

Your job, before this book is over, is to find what *your* portrait of leadership looks like.

But first, let's hear some more sea stories and salty advice . . .

CHAPTER 7

MORE SEA STORIES

⚓

> I, _____, do solemnly swear that I will support and defend the Constitution of the United States against all enemies, foreign and domestic; that I will bear true faith and allegiance to the same; that I take this obligation freely, without any mental reservation or purpose of evasion; and that I will well and faithfully discharge the duties of the office on which I am about to enter. So help me God.
>
> —OATH OF OFFICE OF AN AMERICAN OFFICER,
> TITLE 5, *U.S. CODE*

MAKING MISTAKES

As a new lieutenant serving on a naval base staff, I received a call from my chief of staff directing me to arrange an appointment between CAPT Cook (not his real name) and the admiral. The appointment was an opportunity for the admiral to confront the captain about his drinking problem following a recent drunk-driving arrest. CAPT Cook was angry when he learned why I was calling despite my intent to be as polite and as soft-spoken as possible. He denied having a problem with alcohol and did not want to see the admiral to discuss his drinking. He asked my name and then begrudgingly agreed to meet with the admiral at the designated time. The captain's reaction left me shaken when I hung up the phone.

> When the general lays on unnecessary projects,
> everyone is fatigued.
>
> —*Chen Hao*

Fifteen minutes later the phone rang. It was the admiral and he was laughing hysterically. He said, "Lieutenant, are you aware that there at two CAPT Cooks on this base? You called the wrong one!" He was belly-laughing. I later learned that I called the one with the squeaky-clean reputation.

I was so embarrassed I didn't know what to say, but the admiral smoothed everything over when he collected himself and said calmly, "The only people who don't make mistakes are the people who don't do anything." He went on to say that it took a lot of courage to call the captain under those circumstances. He reassured me that I was doing a great job on his staff and that he didn't want me to ever slow down or to second-guess myself after such an error.

Throughout my thirty-year career, I quietly passed along the admiral's comment to dozens of young officers at the height of their humiliation: "The only people who don't make mistakes are the people who don't do anything." Moral: Don't ever stop pushing, and when mistakes are made, remember this phrase!

—*CDR Kyle Kaker, USN*

THE WARFIGHTER XO

Be professionally competent! Early in my executive officer (XO) tour on an Aegis cruiser, I was up in combat information center (CIC) to observe a combat systems training scenario. A master chief operations specialist was coordinating it, along with the combat systems officer. The master chief says, "Hey XO, do you want to be tactical action officer (TAO) for this scenario?" (The TAO makes the shooting decisions and fights the ship.) I had been a combat systems officer twice (but not on an Aegis ship), and I had just finished my XO training pipeline. That training included a very good course on the Aegis combat system, including significant time training as a TAO in challenging scenarios. So, I felt very confident in my TAO skills and said, "Sure, let's go."

Who hath not served cannot command.

—*Florio*

I then ran a very complex, multimission scenario including control of multiple fighter aircraft against multiaxis attacks. I really felt like I was "in the zone" and orchestrated the entire combat team with crisp orders over our internal net/headphone system. At the end, I called the team together and did a quick debrief of the event. Two nights later I was up briefing the CO on 8 o'clock reports and he said, "The master chief was up yesterday and said the ship is abuzz about this new, super-warfighter XO that we have." I had great warfighting credibility for the rest of my tour.

Moral: Be professionally competent! If you're going to be a good leader at sea on a complex warship, you have to know your stuff.

—*RADM Kevin Quinn, USN*

WHERE THERE'S A WILL . . .

When I was a lieutenant I was the electrical officer on a cruiser. We had been at sea for a few weeks, and we pulled into a port within driving distance of our homes for about a twenty-four-hour stop. When we arrived, the shore power cables on the pier were in complete disarray. These enormous extension cords weighed hundreds of pounds each, and to shut down the ship's power plant to allow us to go home, we had to connect to shore power. Normally there were specialized cranes that could lift the cables and feed them up to the higher level of the cruiser where they were connected. But on the evening of our arrival, there was no crane and the cords were tangled and lying in bunches all over the pier. Our chief electrician took one look and said it was impossible, that there was no way we'd get on shore power that evening, and he promptly retired to the chiefs' mess. The rest of the engineering department quickly fell into one of two groups—those staying on the ship, who didn't really care if we were on shore power or ship's power, and those who could get home to visit their spouses and families during our extremely brief shore visit, *if* we could get on shore power. I was in the latter group, and we decided we were going to pull shore power that evening, even if we had to do it by hand.

It is always well to moor your ship with two anchors.

—*Publilius Syrus, 50 BC*

We rigged lights on the pier. We had the galley gang bring peanut butter and jelly sandwiches. We got about fifty crewmembers out on the pier—Sailors and officers—and we put on gloves, and we pulled and grunted and untangled giant thousand-pound birds nests of shore power cables. After we worked a while, others joined, either out of sympathy or boredom or because they realized we might actually make it work. After several hours of backbreaking labor, we hauled enough cables to energize the ship from the shore, and we shut down the engineering plant. I declared liberty for those not on duty, and we all scampered home for one full night with our families before we got under way again the next day.

I learned a basic truth—that where there's a will, there's a way. I learned that one person can motivate others, and that enough motivated people, working as a team, can do just about anything, even something that others deem impossible.

Pulling shore power cables might be a mundane example, but I've remembered that evening of exertion throughout my career, whenever somebody tells me that something can't be done.

—*RADM Robert Wray, USN*

THE (REALLY) YOUNG SAILOR

As a new ensign on my first ship, we were getting ready to leave for a six-month Mediterranean deployment. Five days before we left, I was reassigned to take over 1st Division, the largest division on the ship, with thirty-eight boatswain's mates and unrated personnel. We handled all deck evolutions, from mooring and anchoring the ship, to small boat and flight deck operations.

After a few days at sea, we moored in Rota, Spain, and set about our daily routine. We received new supplies and a couple of new Sailors. I was in my stateroom when my chief knocked on the door and explained there was an "issue" with one of my new Sailors that needed my immediate attention. He brought him in. I could immediately see there was a problem.

An admiral has to be put to death now and then
to encourage the others.

—Voltaire

This young Sailor looked to be only thirteen, maybe fourteen years old. I asked him to sit down and introduced myself to him and asked where he was from and the normal perfunctory questions you would ask on a first interview. After the first couple of questions, this young Sailor broke down and started crying when I asked him how old he was. He first told me he was seventeen and had his parents' permission to enter the Navy. In my gut, I knew that was wrong, so I asked him two or three times until he finally admitted that he used his older brother's birth certificate to enter the Navy. He explained to me that he was born and raised in a small mining town in the hills of West Virginia. He joined the Navy to escape the poverty of his town, so he could do something better with his life.

He also said that his first real shoes he ever owned were his boondockers he received in boot camp. He then went on to tell me to my utter amazement and shock that he was married and that his wife was thirteen years old, pregnant, and waiting for him in Norfolk. He told me that the Navy recruiter promised him shore duty as a SEABEE and that he could get terrific medical care. I was astounded and amazed, but knew I needed to take some quick actions to take care of this young man, since we were leaving for the Med the next morning.

This was my first real leadership test. What do to with this young man? I had an idea.

My department head was off the ship, to I took the Sailor to the XO and explained the situation. I left him there and went on base to get the base chaplain, who I had known when he was stationed in the states. The chaplain was a captain and could make things happen. He came to the ship, took the young Sailor, and said he'd take care of him in Naval Station Rota, Spain, while the administrative discharge process took place. Discharging him would be in the best interest of the Navy, the young Sailor, and his young bride. After he left the ship, the XO thanked me for thinking "out of the box" to fix a problem.

About five months later during the deployment, I received a letter, handwritten in pencil and very broken English, from this former young Sailor who told me that he was now back in West Virginia with his young bride. He was now working in the mines after the Navy discharged him, and the Navy let him keep his boondockers. He wanted to thank me for all my help in getting him back to his young wife, and he told me that he was expecting his first child in the next month. I never heard from him again.

—*CAPT Bill Malloy, USN*

FIRST TIME THROUGH THE STRAIT OF MALACCA

I was a brand-new third mate fresh out of the Academy. My first job was sailing on an APL C-5A Mariner class. We were sailing from Seattle to ports in the Far East. Our eastbound route would eventually take us to Singapore and the Strait of Malacca. Just a month prior to our departure, another APL ship had run hard aground at the entrance to the strait due to navigational error. It happened during the junior third mate's watch. Both the junior third mate and the captain were fired after an inquiry. Before the end of my first day on the ship, our 6-foot, 6-inch intimidating captain slid a copy of the grounding inquiry under my cabin door. Across the front page, he wrote in bold red ink "THIS WILL NOT HAPPEN ON MY SHIP—BE PREPARED." I began my preparation by praying to God that I would not be on watch when we sailed through the strait!

A leader has the ability to recognize a problem
before it becomes an emergency.

—*Arnold H. Glasgow*

As the days at sea rolled by, I found myself making one rookie mistake after another and drawing the unwanted attention of the captain and crew. Things were not going well for me; by the time we arrived in Singapore, the captain had little confidence in my ability. After several days of cargo operations in Singapore, I realized to my horror that I would indeed be on watch as we departed Singapore and transited through the Strait of Malacca. After more prayer, I realized that the only way to assure a navigational error-free passage was to literally memorize every navigational light, buoy, number, and course on the chart of the strait. That is exactly what I did. Since the captain had no confidence in me, he informed me that he would be standing my watch with me, observing my navigation while he maintained the conn. The Strait of Malacca is a notoriously dangerous passage highlighted by One Fathom Bank. My effort to memorize all navigational aides, land and sea, plus courses, put me in good shape right up to One Fathom Bank. At that point, something went wrong with my navigation; my plot and fix showed the ship heading far too close to the shoal. With great trepidation I informed the captain. He walked back to the chart, looked down at my work, and snarled at me, "Do it again." By now the pilot was away and we were quickly closing on One Fathom Bank. The chart was now a mess as the sweat from my hands had begun to smear the fixes I was attempting to lay down.

Finally after being told three times to recheck my fixed bearings and plot, with my stomach churning, I stood squarely in front of the captain and asked him to please take a round of bearings as I could not find my mistake. He was furious but quickly complied in the chart room as I stood next to the helmsmen. That was the longest three minutes of my early career. The captain never came out of the chart room. I heard his booming voice call out, "Third mate you are correct. Change course to such and such degrees and maintain till the next course change that I have set on the chart. I will be in my cabin. If you have any further questions, don't hesitate to call."

To my astonishment, the captain left me on the bridge with the conn. My navigation was correct; we were going to pass dangerously close to One Fathom Bank. My relationship with the captain and crew changed dramatically from that moment on. And I learned one of the greatest lessons of my seagoing career: "Be Prepared" through prudent seamanship and constant vigilance.

—*CAPT Grant Livingstone, First Class Pilot, Unlimited Tonnage*

POSITIVE LEADERSHIP: NOT ALWAYS THE BEST?

My first class year at the Naval Academy was what one would expect—anticipation of graduation and entering the Navy as an ensign. I was lucky enough to be a varsity athlete, lettering in cross-country, indoor track, and outdoor track.

But running three seasons each academic year was particularly demanding, and the level of training and competition prevented me from participating in company intramural sports and biweekly marching practices and parades. My company classmates didn't seem to mind because we were all close friends. Although I didn't participate in company competitions in intramural sports and marching, each varsity athlete would bring in an additional fifteen points for color company competition for each letter earned, so they felt I was contributing to the company in my own way.

Unfortunately the same degree of consideration and forgiveness was not found in my company officer, LT M. He did not like the fact that I often could not be found in the company area and that I did not participate in company competitions like marching. He also disliked the fact that my dorm room was always less squared away than those of my company mates.

The crowd will follow a leader who marches twenty steps in advance; but if he is a thousand steps in front of them, they do not see and do not follow him.

—*Georg Brandes*

My roommate was a varsity football player. Since both of us were required to work out in our respective sports twice a day, we constantly had wet gym shorts, shirts, socks, and sweat gear to contend with. So we bought a wooden clothes rack, which we hung with daily workout gear and kept in our room's shower stall.

This became a particular sore spot for LT M, because the drying rack filled with workout clothes was not authorized by the Academy and was thus called "gear adrift." In addition it was normally a source of a bad odor, no matter how much we tried to cover it up with deodorant and Polo cologne. Each day we would come back from classes before football and track practices to find an inspection form with a grade of unsatisfactory on it. This often led to a "Form 2" and demerits.

One day the LT summoned me to his office. He began to recite my senior year demerits and informed me that they were going to negatively affect my military performance grades (also known as "grease"). He said this would have a bad effect on my class rank and my assignment after graduation.

He also mentioned that he didn't think I was taking my military training seriously. When I asked for details he said that he had reviewed the company's records and noticed that I had not "fried" anyone (placed them on report) during my first class year.

I was concerned about his comments and asked if there was anything I could do. He told me that if I "fried" someone then he might reconsider my grade.

The next day, after lunch, I went to see him. I brought with me a Form 2 demonstrating that I had finally fried someone. When I told him that I had finally placed a midshipman on report, LT seemed happy to see me for once, because I had taken our last conversation together so seriously. When I handed him the Form 2 and he read it, he suddenly became angry. He loudly protested that my name was on it and demanded an explanation.

I told him I had taken his comments seriously about leadership the day before. I explained that my leadership style was somewhat different from his, as I put a premium on positive leadership and chose to lead by example instead of frying Sailors into doing the right thing. I told him that I was five minutes late for noon meal formation and so felt compelled to fry myself based on his mentoring discussion the previous day.

I was summarily dismissed. Unfortunately, the LT was true to his word, and my grease suffered that semester.

The moral of the story: positive leadership is preferred, but it has its time and place.

—*RADM Chris Paul, USN*

THE DIRTY LAUNDRY

My first fleet job was as a LT (jg) pilot. I was new to the squadron and assigned to the maintenance department. I was flying and was in the office when I wasn't in the air. I was a branch head—I had only one subgroup of the one hundred maintainers in the squadron.

I had a master chief as my branch chief petty officer (CPO). A less naïve individual would have wondered why a master chief was a branch CPO and not the leading CPO of the entire department. Because of flight schedules, twelve-hour missions, and detachments for several days at a time, I was seldom in the office; I relied heavily on the chief to tell me how things were going and what needed to be done. Of course the answer was always that everything was under control. Over time I got to know many of the thirty or so troops in our branch; one flew on my crew. None of course was going to tell the mostly absent LT (jg) about the dirty laundry. Only after we didn't do very well on an annual maintenance inspection did I find out that if I wasn't aboard, the chief was gone. He'd go to the club by 10 a.m. and be drunk not long after that. He was a functional alcoholic so when I did see him, he seemed like a solid, low-key fellow who knew his job. I didn't have enough savvy to ask all the right questions.

To a large extent, leaders get paid to solve problems and get results.

—*Gordy Curphy*

So what is the leadership lesson? First, for the rookie, don't try to reinvent the wheel. Ask for guidance from someone senior enough to provide it. Asking for education is not a sign of weakness. People love to be asked for their opinion; seek them out. Sometimes it is hard to know what it is that you don't know, but you sure won't find out quickly if you don't ask a lot of questions.

Second, pay attention, and do the job you're assigned to do. I wanted to fly; I viewed my maintenance job as a lesser priority. If I had paid more attention to that job, which too was important, I would have recognized the master chief's problems earlier.

And third, if there's dirty laundry, expose it! The senior officers in the squadron knew about the master chief and his drinking problem. They should have warned me, the new guy. Better yet, they should have been dealing with it before I showed up. Not letting the rookie know did a disservice to the enlisted Sailors in the branch.

—*RADM Casey Coane, USN*

BUILDING ESPRIT DE CORPS

While I served as strike officer aboard USS *Milius* in 2000, we had just transited the Strait of Hormuz for the final time, on our way home to San Diego, when the USS *Cole* was bombed by terrorists off the coast of Yemen. After six extremely tense hours stopped dead in the water (DIW) in the Gulf of Oman, we were told to turn around and re-transit the strait, where we spent the next forty-five days back inside the gulf with a daily mission status of "To Be Determined." Our deployment was originally scheduled to return to San Diego right before Thanksgiving, but as Thanksgiving neared, we still had no idea how long we'd be extended. As you can imagine, morale was deteriorating, and there was not much we could tell our friends and family on when we'd be heading home. Finally, after weeks of waiting, we were ordered home to San Diego, scheduled to arrive December 23.

Character is doing the right thing when nobody's looking.

—J. C. Watts

Since we were arriving so close to Christmas, I thought that we should do something special. In the wardroom one evening I suggested to the captain that when we manned the rails at sea and anchor detail we should have everyone wear Santa hats and play Christmas music over the ship's announcing system (1MC). The rest of the wardroom, mostly male, groaned and said that it wasn't manly. The supply officer, of course, said that it would be impossible to get three hundred Santa hats, that it would be too expensive, and that he didn't have time to contract it out; he used every other excuse possible. However after several days of pitching my idea, the captain finally told the suppo to "make it happen." The Santa hats were purchased and loaded on board during our fuel stop in Hawaii. I will never forget how fun and exciting it was to come around the bend under the Coronado Bay Bridge, perfectly clear blue sky with a warm Santa Ana breeze, with everyone topside in dress blues and bright red Santa hats blasting "Santa Claus Is Coming to Town" through the 1MC. The families loved it, the kids were so excited, and it was such a simple and easy gesture.

Moral: Sometimes it's necessary to push past the naysayers to help build esprit de corps. The little things really do matter and can do wonders for crew morale. To this day, I still remember how special it was the day "Boats" blew the whistle, shouted "Moored," and two Sailors in Santa hats shifted colors.

—*LCDR Nicole Maver-Shue, USN*

THE SAILOR AND HIS SON

Being tested in theory and being tested face to face are worlds apart. I found that out one day as I served as an ensign stationed aboard the USS *Preble* (DDG-46). We were steaming off the Falkland Islands during its war with Argentina; the stakes were high and the needs were great as our ship stood at the ready to move into combat, when and if necessary. I was in charge of the seventy Sailors in the Boilers Division, ranging in age from seventeen to fifty-three; I wanted the team to stay tight for this important operation.

> It is happier to be sometimes cheated than not to trust.
>
> —*Samuel Johnson*

One of my Sailors, a boiler technician 3rd class, came to see me privately. He was upset; his five-year-old son had fallen off of a swing set at a playground and broken his left hip. The boy was rushed to a local hospital where emergency surgery would have to insert rods and pins into his bones. The petty officer went on to say that he was divorced and did not have custody of his son because he was in the Navy on sea duty. He said the incident was affecting his work and focus on the job at hand. I continued to listen to him as his voice wavered and a look of helplessness encompassed him. It was clear that coming to me had been a difficult decision under the circumstances. As my Sailor concluded our private conversation, he then shared the underlying, lump-in-his-throat reason that he had come to speak with me—his son had a rare bone disease that caused brittle bones.

What's an ensign to do? I began an internal balancing test: supporting my Sailor might make my department head boss unhappy, because of the importance of the mission. Not supporting my Sailor meant keeping my division intact, but potentially risking mistakes and errors in judgment, due to distraction. I found myself reaching deep down inside to do the right thing. I made the decision to send my Sailor home to be with his son. I felt that his son would not remember the mission we were on in years to come but would remember that his father was by his bedside when he recovered from his surgery. I was committed to this Sailor, as I was to all my Sailors, to do what was right in a time of need, even when the mission might be impacted and even when I, as an ensign, was being tested.

As we know, tests provide feedback. When my Sailor returned, he made it a point to let me know that he held a debt of gratitude. He gave me his total commitment and would do whatever was needed to support me. He rejoined the other Sailors in the division with a renewed focus, sharing that the ensign was someone who cared. Sometimes it's tough to balance the mission and the people. I believe the answer rests, as it did here with my Sailor on that day, in taking care of our people in order to take care of our missions.

—*RDML Kelvin N. Dixon, USN*

SAFETY FIRST

Military Sealift Command is a huge organization with more than a hundred ships. A couple years ago we had a shipboard accident with a man-lift that killed two people; they weren't following proper procedures. After the accident, we spent considerable time re-educating our ten thousand people around the world on safety issues, particularly with man-lifts.

During that period, I spent a lot of time on our ships talking to our mariners. As I always do, I left them my e-mail address in case they had any concerns they didn't want to talk about in the large group. A few days later, I got an e-mail from an experienced mariner who had seen a man-lift on a nearby frigate operating in the same unsafe manner that had caused our accident years before. "I have a son the age of those Sailors on that lift," he wrote. "It would be sad to see anything happen to them, like it did to our guys."

There are no office hours for leaders.

—*Cardinal James Gibbons*

He was afraid to bring up the safety issue to the frigate's crew, because he thought an outsider from another ship commenting on their safety practices would be unwelcome. I told our mariner that it was everybody's responsibility to bring up safety issues, and that I was positive the frigate's skipper would be happy to get any feedback he could to make his crew more safe. I called the commodore, who called the frigate's captain, and relayed the issue about the man-lift. Sure enough, they were glad that our mariner had seen the issue and had reported it (even if he used an unusual routing to report it!).

Moral: Some things, like safety, are just too important to worry about protocol and hurting people's feelings. You've heard the phrase "Everybody is a safety observer." It's true. If anybody sees anybody doing something unsafe, particularly with something that can kill people, they should report it. And damn the consequences.

—*RADM Robert Wray, USN*

KNOW YOUR GEAR, AND MAKE IT WORK!

As a lieutenant during Desert Storm I was assigned to the U.S. Mine Countermeasures Group in the Northern Arabian Gulf clearing the 1,200 mines that had been laid by the Iraqis. I was a liaison officer to the Japanese Maritime Self-Defense Force that sent six ships to help in the mine-clearing effort. Our ships had found a mine that we had never encountered before, and we needed to perform an "exploitation" in order to learn more about this device. The explosive ordinance disposal (EOD) divers who conducted this evolution—never done before on a live weapon—used their normal procedures. This included attaching lifting bags that fill with air to raise the mine so it can be beached for full investigation. This was a large weapon, so large that when the lifting bags were filled and the mine started to rise, the bags broke and the mine settled back on the bottom.

With no options I set my mind to figuring out a way to make this happen. I was very familiar with all the various equipment at our disposal. Determining that we needed more lifting power, plus the ability to rig the device for towing, I proposed that we use the "O" floats. These O, or Oropesa, floats are normally used for towing mechanical minesweeping gear through the water. Since the lifting bags could get the mine off the bottom, but not hold them or make them towable, I suggested that the EOD divers lift the mine with the bags and then transfer the rig to the O floats. Those floats were designed for towing and much more stable and reliable. It worked!

Moral: As a young officer, know your gear, be resourceful, and make suggestions. Technical savvy and ingenuity will make you stand out as a leader.

—CAPT Arthur Stauff, USN

> To act is easy; to think is hard.
>
> —*Goethe*

KEEP YOUR BOSS INFORMED

This is my favorite no-kidding story. I'd told it repeatedly to my military and civilian troops over the years (making this a parable, I suppose), and every single person understood the moral. Here it is:

Once as a young main propulsion assistant (MPA) ensign on a destroyer, the commanding officer (CO) climbed down into my engine room around 0500 just after we threw a thrust bearing on the main shaft. When he asked, "How's it going?" I filled him in on the casualty. But now I had a significant problem: the CO knew about a major casualty but my boss, the chief engineer (CHENG), did not. The CO's shoes were not even out of sight as I was calling the CHENG in his stateroom. He was not pleased to get a phone call at 0515 and definitely not pleased to learn about the thrust bearing. I learned later that no sooner had he hung up his phone than the CO called him, asking "How's it going?" The CHENG was able to respond with information about the casualty, looking good to his boss.

> An army of deer led by a lion is more to be feared than an army of lions led by a deer.
>
> —*Chabrias*

The moral of the story is to keep your chain of command informed, especially when the chain gets jumped unexpectedly. I was so impressed with this lesson that it is to this day one of my guiding principles.

—*LT David Wyatt, USN*

THE TWO-DAY LEADERSHIP LESSON

I was a young, twenty-six-year-old LT (jg), newly assigned as damage control assistant in USS *Omaha* (SSN 692). We were conducting one of those "special operations of great importance to the defense of the United States," which is a fancy way of saying we were on an important mission where (a) we had to have continuous submarine coverage, (b) we could not transmit, and (c) if we were forced to leave station, another submarine would have to be sent in to replace us. In other words, we couldn't screw up. And as usually happens during a mission of that duration, Murphy raised his head. This time it was in the form of a ship's service hydraulic power plant accumulator leak—a large and complex piece of equipment that usually was repaired by an intermediate maintenance activity (IMA) and not the ship's crew. Fortunately my leading petty officer (LPO) had served shore duty in an IMA and had conducted several similar repairs. After analyzing the failure with him, I went forward to give the captain the good news and the bad news. The bad news: The accumulator would have to be taken off service for several hours, if not days. The good news: We were fairly confident we could actually repair it at sea—we would not have to leave station. The captain gave us permission to start the repair.

Reason and calm judgment, the qualities specially belonging to a leader.

—*Tacitus*

Upon reporting aboard *Omaha*, I had resolved to myself that I would always be a "deckplate leader" during this tour, so I figured this would be the time to start demonstrating that leadership. In other words I vowed to "hang" with my mechanics and provide whatever assistance I could with the repairs. In so doing I also figured I could learn a thing or two about the construction and maintenance of the hydraulic plant. My boss, the chief engineer, was also a frequent visitor during the activity. He'd check up on how things were going, ask if we needed any more assistance, then pretty much disappear. Disassembly of a large hydraulic accumulator was a complex affair in the best of conditions; in the cramped spaces of a submarine engine room it was particularly taxing. Heavy components and piping had to be rigged out without damaging fragile electronics, small pieces had to be inventoried and tagged, quality assurance documents had to be prepared, and the whole site had to be kept clean to standards. The disassembly effort took the better part of a day, and my LPO remained on station supervising during the entire affair. All my Sailors vowed to stay awake until the job was done, and thinking this would be a good learning experience for them, I let them.

But Murphy wasn't done with us yet. Reassembling the accumulator seals proved to be nearly impossible. Dozens of small ball bearings had to be inserted in the housing, then the entire assembly put together without losing a single ball bearing. Several of our younger, "steady hand" mechanics tried to get the assembly pieced together without luck. Even I gave it a shot—no joy. Our LPO, unusually calm and unflappable, would try time after time, only to have the ball bearings fall out at the last possible moment. This became a mind-numbing, agonizing, repetitive drill.

Finally, after about thirty hours of continuous work without sleep, eating in shifts, and taking short breaks when we could, the accumulator was reassembled and it was time to leak-check the device. We pressurized it, and *wham!*—it leaked worse than before. My division's disappointment was understandable, but was magnified a hundredfold by the extreme fatigue brought on by over a day of continuous work. Now the problem was worse than before, and my guys were too exhausted to do anything about it. This was without a doubt the hardest report I had ever brought to my captain in my still-new submarine career. The only thing I could do was tell my guys to secure the accumulator, isolate the leak, shut that side of the plant down (again), and get some rest so we could regroup. My own sense of personal guilt was nearly intolerable. So while my guys were sleeping, I went over the system drawings again to see if I could figure out what went wrong. Then I remembered something I had heard months before—that the engineering yeoman who maintains the ship's drawings was way behind in updating our files. So on a hunch, I went to the ship's microfiche index to see what version of the drawings we should have been using. And sure enough—I discovered that the plans we were using during the repair had been superseded. And when I printed out the new drawings, it turned out we had used the wrong seal on the accumulator. It had leaked because we installed the wrong part. Should my LPO have figured this out before we started the repairs? Of course. But I was the division officer and it was my responsibility. While my zeal to exhibit "deckplate leadership" was appropriate (and would continue to serve me well in later years), it did not absolve me of the responsibility to be the division officer.

It is priceless to find a person who will take responsibility, who will finish and follow through to the final detail—to know when someone has accepted an assignment that it will be effectively, conscientiously completed.

—Richard L. Evans

So while I was "hanging" with my guys, nobody was doing that "officer stuff" I should have been doing—checking to ensure we were using the right drawings and procedures, that the right parts were being used, that proper precautions were being followed, and that the job would get done right.

Part of this dynamic was caused by the fact that my LPO was way older and more experienced than I was. That caused me to trust him perhaps more than I should have. Heck, he was almost thirty-five! Part of it was a desire to be "liked" by my guys, to prove I was just "one of the boys," no different than they were (one of the reasons I rarely wore my academy class ring before I became more senior). But the bottom line is this: I let my guys work nonstop for almost two days in an effort to conduct a repair that was rendered futile by my failure to do my job. It was my fault that their work had been wasted. It was my fault the final repair would be delayed by more than two days. This was a lesson I would never forget.

My service in the Navy continued through chief engineer, through executive officer, through captain, even through commodore. And over the years, I witnessed many repairs similar to the one I experienced on *Omaha*. And every now and then, I would see a young division officer hovering around the technicians just like I did. And when I did, I would always pull that young officer aside and ask him one question: "What should you be doing right now to make sure this work will not be wasted effort?"

—*CAPT William Toti, USN*

TAKE CARE OF MY PEOPLE

My first leadership lesson I learned from a chief petty officer shortly after my commissioning at Navy Reserve Officers Training Corps Unit at Rensselaer Polytechnic Institute. I was checking out with Yeoman Chief Williams. She said, "Ensign Blumberg, I have all your paperwork sorted and ready for your departure. All of your midshipman paperwork is in this folder and you can do whatever you want with it. In this folder is your service record and other required documentation, which you need to present when you check into your next command."

> To the timid and hesitating, everything is impossible
> because it seems so.
>
> —*Walter Scott*

As she handed me these two folders and I tried to grab them, she brought them back to her and replied, "Just remember, take care of my people." She then handed me the folders and said, "Have a nice day and good luck in the Fleet." After ten years of active duty service and currently serving as a commanding officer, I still vividly remember her words. If we don't take care of our shipmates, we have no ship. If we do not take care of our people, then we have no Navy.

> —*LCDR Gary Blumberg, USN*

NOT HAVING THE ANSWERS

As a member of shipboard fighter squadrons for many years, I saw many commanding officers (COs) come and go. All of them had an Officers Call on their first day in the job, but I can't say I remember what any of them said, except for one. One CO stood up in front of the ready room and said, "I know I'm in charge, but don't think I have all the answers." He struck a chord with me that I remember to this day, some fifteen years later. In fact I have used those same words during each one of my four command tours.

> The man who trusts men will make fewer mistakes
> than he who distrusts them.
>
> —*DiCavour*

With that one short sentence, that skipper set the tone for his highly successful tour in two ways. First, he created a command climate where new ideas and discussion were encouraged. He essentially said, "You people will know things I don't know, and I want those ideas." Second, he made all of us in the ready room feel that we could make a contribution and be part of the solution. What a great way to build a *team*! We all know the Navy is a military organization and the boss has 51 percent of the vote, but when people in a command get to have input and feel that their input is given due consideration, they will feel valued and more likely to support wholeheartedly the boss's final decision.

Most of us have worked, at some point in our careers, in an environment where our boss says, "If I want your opinion I'll ask you. You job is to be seen but not heard." How did that make us feel? Did that stifle our desire to propose new ideas? Did we feel part of the team? One simple sentence, followed up by action, can create a positive atmosphere that encourages collaboration and team building and ultimately leads to mission success.

Moral: When you get to your ships, tell them: "I know I'm in charge, but I don't think I have all the answers." Your people will be glad you did.

—*RDML John Sadler, USN*

START TOUGH, THEN BACK OFF

When I was a new ensign I was sent to my first ship and assigned a division. When I arrived, my division was a mess. They didn't have a chief petty officer (CPO) in charge, and the division suffered from a lack of discipline and leadership. I came in as the nice-guy officer who tried to lead through example, through consensus, and through discussing things with the group. The division soon branded me as a patsy, and despite my best efforts to cajole them into better performance, nothing much happened. They were known as the "dirtbag" division.

Halfway through my first deployment with this gang, a CPO was finally assigned to us. He flew in during a port call and spent the first couple days on board in the chiefs' mess, getting the scoop on me and each member of the division. To this day, thirty years later, I still remember the first time we met him as we stood out at quarters on the flight deck, under way in cold weather. I shook his hand and introduced him to the division. He promptly launched into a tirade about what a mess we were. He yelled. He stomped. He inspected each member of the division and spat out corrections on hair, uniform, shoes, posture, insignia. He announced out loud every bad thing he had heard from the chiefs' mess about each one of us. Frankly he scared me to death, and I was technically his boss. I could see the Sailors in the division stiffen with fear—a new sheriff was clearly in town, and boy, was he frightening!

> An officer is much more respected than any other man
> who has little money.
>
> —*Samuel Johnson*

For the next forty-eight hours or so, the new chief ran the division ragged. All new haircuts. Shined shoes. Lengthy lectures at quarters. Pressed uniforms. Corrections to watch-standing. Seabag inspections. Berthing cleanups. No TV or movies—just work. He scared the bejesus out of the division and worked them like they had never been worked before. I stayed away as much as I could.

And after forty-eight hours, it stopped—like it gets calm after a storm has passed through. The chief became his normal self—a mild, humorous, gentle man. For his next three years on board, I never again saw him get angry or raise his voice. But the division had gotten the message—they saw what he could be, and that was enough. From that day forward, they marched to his drummer—they met his standards, they obeyed him without question. Most important, the division became measurably better in every way.

The lesson I learned is that when a new boss starts off gentle and conciliatory, some may interpret it as weakness.

And that once you start off gently, it's hard to become the tough guy. I learned that it's better to start as the tough guy to set the standards high, and then back off.

—*RADM Robert Wray, USN*

MAN OVERBOARD!

In January 2003 I was commanding officer of USS *John F. Kennedy* (CV67). We had just completed a lengthy major overhaul and were scheduled for a five-day at-sea period for post-availability sea trials. The flight deck was not yet certified for flight operations, and no helicopter support detachment for search and rescue would be available for our sea trials. This meant that I would be restricted to a boat recovery in the event of a man overboard situation. The weather forecast was generally favorable, but with periods of unusually heavy seas and high winds. These conditions would make small-boat operations impossible. I decided that we would proceed to sea under these conditions, despite the potential risk.

Nothing is stronger than habit.

—*Ovid*

After two days of routine sea trial events, I signed my night orders and noted that the strengthening wind and increasing seas would make night boat operations hazardous if not impossible. I spoke to my command team and then addressed the crew on the 1MC, cautioning them that I had limited options for man overboard recovery, and I directed the closure of weather decks to all nonessential personnel.

At roughly 2 a.m., my worst nightmare was realized with the call "Man overboard, starboard side, away the ready lifeboat!" I was quickly joined on the bridge by my executive officer (XO) as we maneuvered to create a lee for possible boat deployment. My first lieutenant called from the starboard sponson aft to report the rigid hull inflatable boat (RHIB) and crew ready to be lowered into the water. Given the weather conditions I was reluctant to put the boat and its eight-Sailor crew at risk in a nasty sea. As I was deliberating, the XO looked me right in the eye and said, "Captain, we have a report of two lights going over the starboard side into the water. The lookout was unable to determine if there were bodies attached to those lights." Then came the most chilling report of all: "Captain, we have two men missing from muster. Both were seen on the flight deck, starboard side, moments before the lights were seen going overboard."

I now had two good reasons to believe I had two crewmembers in the water. Their survival time, given ambient temperatures and high winds, was less than an hour, even if they had good flotation. There was no helicopter rescue option. If there were men in the water, only my boat and rescue crew could recover them. Every moment that I delayed a decision to deploy the rescue boat lowered the survivability chances of my two missing crew. On the other hand, dare I risk eight Sailors in an attempt to rescue two? How could I *not* take that risk, knowing two were in peril on the sea?

I asked for professional advice from the XO and first lieutenant. First replied, "We can do this Captain! Let us go get our guys!" Of course, the First was looking at relatively calm seas created by the lee of a 90,000-ton aircraft carrier. From the bridge the XO and I could see the true wind strength and increasingly choppy seas outside of the ship's lee. I made my decision in seconds: "First lieutenant, lower the boat."

No sooner had I received the report "Boat is away, Captain," when the XO rushed to me to report, "Captain, all crew members now sighted and accounted for!" If I really didn't have a potential tragedy before, I sure had one now, with eight Sailors alone in a small boat on a dark night in angry seas. And I had put them there.

Outside the protection of the carrier's lee, my small boat and eight Sailors were being pounded to pieces. I ordered them to return to the ship for immediate recovery, an order they eagerly obeyed. It took seven unsuccessful approaches before we could get the boat secured to the hoist and raised, but the boat was eventually recovered safely.

I greeted the crew as they came off the boat. They were soaked to the skin, freezing cold, and absolutely terrified. I called them all together because I wanted them to understand why I had risked their lives needlessly. All were respectful, but my search and rescue (SAR) swimmer dropped his gear on the deck, said "I quit," and never stood SAR swimmer duty again.

Despite making logical, defendable decisions each step of the way, in the end I was backed into a corner in which my decision placed eight priceless lives at unacceptable risk. I had made what I thought was the right decision at the time with the information I had. I had every good reason to believe that I had two men in the water when I launched the boat. If that had in fact been true and I had *not* made an attempt to save them, I would have been forever unable to forgive myself for my inaction and would have been worthless as a captain to this ship and crew. In the same situation again, with the same information, I would lower the boat. Even so, to this day I deeply regret placing eight lives at risk over bad information.

What's the leadership lesson? First, you have to understand that what can go wrong, will go wrong. I should have lobbied more strongly for onboard SAR helicopter support. Second, Mother Nature is a merciless lady, never to be underestimated or trifled with. Third, if you do not decide, facts will decide for you. Waiting to gather more information was not an option. If there were men in the water, delay meant possible death. Fourth, and perhaps most importantly, only the senior officer on the scene can make these command decisions, and any officer must be morally prepared to face a choice as I had to. Once the decision is made, it's yours and yours alone. You will be held totally accountable, forever, for choosing wisely—or not. I was lucky and I didn't lose anyone. Nevertheless the decision and its ramifications haunt me to this day. Such is the responsibility and total accountability of leadership at sea.

—*RDML Ronald H. Henderson Jr., USN*

THE ENSIGN IN THE SNOW

My first lesson in leadership and motivating people came just after I graduated from the Naval Academy. While waiting for my start date at Nuclear Power School, I was assigned temporary duty to Portsmouth Naval Shipyard as an assistant ship superintendent to a submarine in overhaul. It was winter in New Hampshire, on the waterfront; it was cold! I was an understudy to a very salty and well-respected limited duty officer (LDO) who was very savvy about getting things done. One night on the graveyard shift, a system had a part failure. It was serious—if not fixed quickly, it would delay the test program and thereby possibly keep the submarine in overhaul longer than planned. I called the supply department and they said they would bring someone in from home to draw the part, and, as long as they had an officer sign for it, the paperwork could be completed the next day.

Shallow men believe in luck. . . .
Strong men believe in cause and effect.

—*Ralph Waldo Emerson*

Before I left to go to the Supply Building across the yard a worker came in and said they had found a way to fix the system without the new part. I sank down in my chair and let out a big sigh of relief, since now I wouldn't have to walk all the way across the snowy shipyard. However, the LDO had other ideas. He said, "Get up right now, hustle across the yard and pick up the part. Thank the supply folks like they were saving your life, and bring back the part. We can turn it back in tomorrow." I protested, not liking in the least the idea of trudging across the yard in the cold and snow. The LDO looked me in the eye and said, "What will they do the next time you call, Ensign?" I learned an important lesson—people will go above and beyond to make things happen, but you better make sure they know their efforts are appreciated if you want it to happen more than once.

—*RDML William Timme, USN*

CHAPTER 8

More Salty Advice

The young American responds quickly and readily to the exhibition of qualities of leadership on the part of his officers. Some of these qualities are industry, energy, initiative, determination, enthusiasm, firmness, kindness, justness, self-control, unselfishness, honor, and courage.

—GEN John Lejeune, commandant
of the Marine Corps

THE FOUR Ps OF LEADERSHIP

I graduated from the Coast Guard Academy in 1982 and started my seagoing career as an ensign on a polar icebreaker, eventually serving twelve years at sea. I was fortunate to command a 140-foot icebreaking tug as a lieutenant, and later, I commanded a 210-foot medium endurance cutter. The following encapsulates my thoughts as a "model," based on a consolidation of my myriad experiences. Hopefully this will help guide junior officers just starting out their careers at sea to develop into successful seagoing leaders. I call these the "Four Ps of Leadership."

1. Performance

- Seagoing services are performance based. You must demonstrate superb performance to execute your ship's missions and to ensure the safety of your shipmates.

- You must perform the very best that you can first and foremost in your primary duty, but also in your collateral duties, regardless of how mundane they might seem.
- Strive to become the "go-to" person for a specific function on your ship.
- People will respect you for your performance, and if you perform well, you will overcome any preconceived notions that your coworkers or supervisors may have had about your capabilities.

The most powerful weapon on earth is the human soul on fire.

—*Field Marshal Ferdinand Foch*

---

2. Preparedness

- Preparation = Performance (see above).
- Always arrive prepared . . . to your new ship, to stand watch, to give a presentation. All it takes to prepare is effort—there is no excuse for not taking the time to prepare.
- If you don't prepare well, you have failed to demonstrate respect for your shipmates and devotion to your duty.
- The Coast Guard motto is Semper Paratus—you can't be "always ready" unless you are prepared.

3. Presentation

- Earn the respect of your subordinates, peers, and superiors. Make this one of your top priorities! Mission execution is not about making friends or being liked, it's about getting the job done in a professional manner.
- The way you present yourself the first day you arrive at your new ship is important. If you present yourself in a professional manner that exudes business, you will

ward off any misperceptions and set yourself up for success.

- Strive to present yourself in a professional, yet approachable manner.
- Be consistent in your presentation day after day; don't make the crew try to guess what your mood is going to be or how you are going to react.

4. Persistence

- When the going gets toughest and you're ready to quit (and there will come a time when you feel this way), be patient and tough it out. People will rotate before you know it, circumstances will change, and you will be stronger for what you have endured.
- Keep trying, even if you fail time and again. You will eventually get it and may even end up better than your peers if you have had to work harder for the result. The consequences of not continuing to try after failing at a tough task are that you will fall short of challenging yourself and therefore will resign yourself to mediocrity. "A mediocre officer is always at his or her best."
- Consider that you can learn more from one "bad" boss than a career full of good ones. Take hardship as an opportunity in this respect. You will learn tolerance, discipline, and restraint; and you will deeply imprint the leadership traits you want to demonstrate as you get more senior.
- Persistence pays huge dividends over time. Be patient.

Most of all, enjoy the incredible opportunity to serve our Nation in a ship at sea. It passes by all too quickly, and the time is yours right now to build the memories, sea stories, friends, and lessons that will influence you for the rest of your life.

—*RDML Sandra Stosz, USCG*

SEVEN COMMANDING OFFICER "HOT" ITEMS

These were seven leadership points I tried to stress to my junior officers when I was commanding officer of a nuclear cruiser:

1. Mission Accomplishment and Mission Readiness. Keep us always ready to do our job. Take care of your people. Train.

2. Watchstanding. Whether on the bridge, quarterdeck, propulsion plant, combat information center, radio, damage control central, be good watchstanders. Ensure you are properly qualified and prepared for the watch. Train your subordinates. Be ready for any emergency responses required by your assignment. Be fully proficient in damage control. Train. The quarterdeck must be impeccable. Formal salutes and presentations. Perfect execution of colors and honors. Greet all hands and be efficient in escorting visitors. Know the boss(es). Train. Ops and bridge watches must be alert, filled with foresight; and always keep me informed. Train. Engineering and propulsion plant watches must remain formal and knowledgeable about the ship's operations. Ship safety and reactor safety must be balanced and your top priorities. Train.

3. Phone talkers' and radio users' manners. Be formal and efficient in phone talking, including outside lines. Answer in a manner that conveys respect for those calling in. Speak clearly and be helpful. Answer all calls promptly. Before you speak over a radio circuit, know what you are going to say. Keep it short, simple, and clear!! Train.

4. Appearance. Keep the ship looking good, inside and out! No rust or unkempt areas. Look at our sides versus others. Damage control material condition includes caps on sound-powered phone jacks and all

hardware in place and secured with lanyard locking pins. All lights should be bright. Maintain quality places to live, eat, study, and relax. Plan and clean the ship every day. Train.

Character is much easier kept than recovered.

—*Thomas Paine*

---

5. Planned Maintenance (PM). Our window to the world. One hundred percent completion of PM items. Work center supervisors see the commanding officer when they don't get all scheduled maintenance done. Really do good maintenance. Check it. Configuration control—learn and follow the rules! Train.
6. Logs and Records. Keep them up to date and accurate. They are your written legacy for how well you do your job. Know the "dead man" rule.[1] Train.
7. Be on Time. Train.

—*CAPT David Brown, USN*

LEADERSHIP SPELLED OUT

L = Loyalty
E = Enthusiasm and Endurance
A = Accountability and Adaptability
D = Dedication and Discipline
E = Empathy
R = Respect
S = Sense of Humor
H = Honor
I = Integrity
P = Professionalism

—*CAPT Richard Jones, USN*

---

[1] The dead man rule prohibits one party in an oral agreement from testifying about the conversation if the other party is deceased. The captain is making the point that in the event of a mishap, the written record will prevail.

I find it fascinating that most people plan their vacations with better care than they plan their lives. Perhaps that is because escape is easier than change.

—*John Rohn*

ASK YOUR FOLKS WHAT THEY THINK

Pay attention to and ask opinions of your subordinates. Doing this has several benefits.

First, as an officer, you cannot know every single thing about each and every task performed by every Sailor under your command. And you shouldn't have to know everything or to be the duty expert on every facet of your unit's mission. As an officer your mission is different, and you should have a broader perspective on things. However, for that Sailor or unlicensed seaman, his entire raison d'être is that piece of equipment or specified task. His piece of your unit's mission is much narrower, and he will probably be the expert in it. So if you have a question in which knowing something about a piece of equipment or a task will help you in your own decision making, ask your subordinates. You will probably get a much more accurate response that will thereby enable you to make a better decision.

Second, by asking for your subordinate's input, you give him a sense of ownership in the mission. The mission is no longer just something thrust down on him from above. If he becomes part and parcel of it, it becomes his mission on an individual level.

You have to go out, but you don't have to come back.

—*U.S. Lifesaving Service*

Third is how your subordinates will view you. Many Sailors tend to look with some degree of suspicion on the abilities of newly minted officers. The concern is that a new officer might make orders that are counterproductive or not in keeping with real-world methods of performing tasks. However, by asking for information that will better enable her to make decisions and issue orders, the officer has shown that she is not just full of bluster; rather, she is honestly seeking the best way to accomplish the mission without being too egotistical to seek the best input available, even if that input might come from the most junior Sailor in the unit. And even if some advice is not ultimately taken by the officer, the Sailors can accept that with the knowledge that their opinions were at least considered, and that she values them as individuals with varied skills and abilities.

—*CAPT Jonathan Brazee, USN*

LEAD BY LETTING OTHERS LEAD

One of the most important rules of effective leadership is to never relinquish unity of command. But command, and control, are different. Control can be elusive. The more you pull at people, the less control you have on their actions. Therefore leadership is less about barking orders and more about subtlety.

And when we think we lead, we are most led.

—*Lord Byron*

Delegation can be a double-edged sword. Delegate poorly and you will fail; delegate the proper amount to the right people and you will succeed. First you must assemble an efficient chain of command that shares your goals and values. You must also look for team members who make up for deficiencies you might have or who have the skills you lack. Abraham Lincoln had virtually no military experience, yet understood the cost of war and the stakes involved. After one too many disappointing generals, he realized his lack of experience and appointed General Grant to lead his Union military machine. Realizing your own limitations but working with others who have the skills you do not can make all the difference.

Finally you must clearly communicate what their mission is and how they fit into the command structure. Once a team has been provided a clear final objective, move away and allow the team to develop its own plan of action. This leverages the creative spirit in your Sailors and your team. Require periodic updates and provide course corrections when needed.

Bottom line: Lead by letting others lead.

—*Senior Chief Matthew Skaggs, USN*

If you teach a man something, he will never learn.

—*George Bernard Shaw*

BE A PERPETUAL STUDENT!

I am both a naval officer and a U.S. Merchant Marine master mariner. Working in both capacities has allowed me to learn to be a good seaman. The Army teaches its officers to be soldiers first; similarly, naval officers should be seamen first. When signed aboard a ship as an officer, learn to be a seaman first and always take the initiative to learn, because every day aboard ship is different.

Don't take the quartermaster's word on where the ship is. Learn to navigate. Don't take the weather report for granted. Learn weather and learn to interpret the changing conditions. Learn about everything that occurs in your surroundings, because this creates optimal situational awareness. Learning as much as possible makes you a better seaman and, therefore, a better officer.

This is leadership by example. Sailors respect a real seaman. I'm a harbor pilot by specialty now, and I also dock ships for the Navy as a reserve officer. While confiding in a senior pilot one day about the challenges of piloting in my waters, he pointedly told me, "Be confident in your knowledge." This is very true and succinct. To be good and safe at your job, you must be a perpetual student.

—*LCDR Alexander Soukhanov, USN*

Educators take something simple and make it complicated.
Communicators take something complicated
and make it simple.

—*John C. Maxwell*

RULES FOR SHIPHANDLING

My rules for "Shiphandling for Officers" also apply in many areas of life beyond shiphandling. Here they are:

- Everyone on board is there to assist the officer of the deck.
- Use all technology available to you, but never underestimate the value of seaman's eye.
- Have a plan, but be ready to adjust.
- Always have a way out; never box yourself in.
- Manage your momentum.
- Give commands taking into account how long it will take for the effect to be observed.
- Verify that your commands are being executed properly.
- There is a time for patience and a time for bold, decisive action—decide what time it is.
- One good command beats ten poor commands.
- Know where your pivot point is.

- She backs into the wind!
- When making less than five knots, there are only two rudder positions: full and amidships.

—*RDML Steven Ratti, USCG*

DELEGATE 'TIL IT HURTS

You must master the art and science of delegation. Delegation is good for a number of reasons:

- It develops your subordinates.
- It frees you to do higher-order, more important work.
- It increases the total throughput of you and your team.
- It builds in you the ability to lead larger teams and organizations.

But for many, delegation is not natural. Too many young officers are reluctant to delegate because they are afraid their subordinates won't do it right. Some underdelegate and try to run the world themselves. Some overdelegate and try to do nothing. Some delegate the wrong things and spend their remaining time on other wrong things.

I wish to have no connection with any ship that does not sail fast, for I intend to go in harm's way.

—*John Paul Jones*

The most common problem, however, is underdelegation, either from fear, or insecurity, or a sense of control, or, sometimes, a sense of ego. Thus I tell young officers that they must "delegate 'til it hurts." In general push tasks down to your subordinates as much as humanly possible, to free up your time to do the things they can't do. How much is enough? You're delegating about right when it starts to hurt. It'll hurt in three ways:

1. You'll feel uncomfortable. You'll wonder if your people can do the task as well as you can.
2. There will be mistakes. But if you aren't delegating enough so that your crew occasionally makes mistakes, then you aren't delegating enough! The key is to ensure the mistakes are small and caught in time. Mistakes are the result of people learning and doing new things.
3. You'll be envious. There will be times when the task is a fun or exciting one, something you'd like to do. But if it's more appropriate for one of your people to do it, suck it up, and delegate! For instance, if a dignitary is visiting the ship and giving your organization an award, you'll want to give the tour and receive the recognition. But, better yet, assign the role to one of your junior people—let her bask in the glory. She will enjoy it and will feel proud for having been given the responsibility.

If you ain't hurtin'—at least a little—then you ain't delegating enough. And if you're not delegating enough, you can never grow to be all the leader you want to be.

—*RADM Robert Wray, USN*

LEADERSHIP THE "RIGHT" WAY

My command philosophy for leadership at sea speaks to the most junior seaman and the most senior officer. The objective is to operate our ship to accomplish the mission effectively, efficiently, and safely. In meeting this goal, there are three primary tenets:

Treat people right. An atmosphere of mutual respect is expected and required. We train people and we mentor them. We tolerate honest mistakes, but do not accept them. We use delegation to get things done and strive to never waste our people's time. The crew, spouses, and dependents are all part of the family—and it is right for us to take care of our family.

Do the right things. At the most basic level, do your job. Take the initiative and do your job without being told. If you do not know what your job is, or how to do it, tell your boss. As you get more senior you must learn to figure out more of your job on your own. All things are not equally important. Leadership at every level has the responsibility to set priorities and state what needs to be done as clearly as necessary.

Do things right. This means more than following procedures and being safe. Give 110 percent when you are on watch. Do things right the first time. Set high standards for yourself and others. Do the right thing even when no one is watching or will ever know. Plan for the best rather than simply hoping for the best. Always look for better ways to do things, and remember good ideas can come from anyone. There is a temptation to do more with less—don't! We play to win, and we do what we can with what we have, and we do it right—effectively, efficiently, and safely.

—*CAPT Scott Minium, USN*

The ear of the leader must ring with the voices of the people.

—*Woodrow Wilson*

REMEMBER YOUR VOICE—BE UNFLAPPABLE

Whether your career is only a few months old, as in the case of most midshipmen or cadets, or whether you're an "old salt," we have all experienced two types: the flamer and the unflappable.

The flamers only know how to make their point with an anger-laced voice. My first memories of my days in the Navy are those of Plebe Summer, the Naval Academy's indoctrination program. One of the most memorable facets of that six-week period was the volume of upperclassmen's voices. First class midshipmen—seniors—critiqued every act, demanding exact correctness at every turn. Failure to perform at the desired standard usually drew a firm but fair rebuke. As a training environment, the Plebe Summer program set the bar for military excellence; it indoctrinated us. The Firsties used loud voices to keep us under pressure. Even then, with everything that was going on around us, my classmates and I were quick to recognize those who could make a point with volume but without malice. And most of us determined which leadership style we would choose to emulate.

All the regulations and gold braid in the Pacific Fleet cannot enforce a sailor's devotion. That, each officer . . . must earn on his own.

—*Arnold S. Lott*

In the operational environment, the flamer's impact is much more profound in that it affects morale and discipline. Consider the example of an operations officer embarked in a Navy destroyer during the 1990s. Tactically capable, a great shiphandler, and intelligent, one would think this officer had it all. However whenever one of his charges, officer and enlisted alike, made an error, that person usually found himself or herself receiving a loud and public berating. His people did their jobs, but nothing more. Rather than gain the respect of those around him, peers and subordinates held him in contempt, and further, ridiculed him in private. In time the Navy chose not to promote him past the rank of commander. However one has to wonder: How many lives and careers did his negative approach to leadership impact?

One of the best leaders I've ever known commanded personnel in two wars, Vietnam and Desert Storm. What made this officer superb was the self-discipline he brought to the task of leading people, both in the field and in the office. He taught that the only time a leader should raise his voice was to save a life, either others or his. He taught that as leaders, our charges have an expectation of unflappability in their leaders, in all things. Further, he espoused that they had a right to that expectation and that if we could not live up to it, then we should not take up the mantle of leadership. One of the most versatile tools we have as leaders is our voice. We can use it to inspire or to cause others to perspire. Shouting angrily typically displays a lack of control of one's emotions. Leaders must give the appearance of being in control, if not of the situation, then certainly of themselves. Words are powerful. Once transmitted, words cannot be recalled. Words spoken in anger or fear are the most powerful and dangerous of all.

—*RDML Ken Carodine, USN*

CHAPTER 9

What Seniors Say: Leadership Advice from the Ages

---⚓---

[Officers,] . . . be strict in your discipline; that
is, to require nothing unreasonable of your
officers and men, but see that whatever is
required be punctually complied with.

Reward and punish every man according
to his merit, without partiality or prejudice;
hear his complaints; if it is well founded,
redress them; if otherwise, discourage them,
in order to prevent frivolous ones.

Discourage vice in every shape, and impress
upon the mind of every man, from the lowest
to the highest, the importance of the cause,
and what it is they are contending for.

—GEN GEORGE WASHINGTON,
IN A LETTER OF INSTRUCTION TO HIS OFFICERS

At this point in this primer on leadership, we've
reviewed thirty-five books representing ten thousand pages of thoughts from dozens of authors.
You saw the survey results of 380 seagoing salts representing
nine thousand years of cumulative experience. You read the
sea stories and bits of advice, all generated from current and
recent seagoing leaders. All worthwhile, hopefully.

But imagine standing in a room with Washington,
Jefferson, Paine, Churchill, Einstein, St. Paul, Carnegie, and
Theodore Roosevelt (among others) and listening to their

leadership advice. Imagine if they were joined by military and naval heroes such as GEN George Patton, John Paul Jones, ADM Arleigh "31-knot" Burke, Nimitz, Eisenhower, and others, and, finally, by thought leaders, CEOs, and philosophers. What might such a group say about leadership?

> In a social order in which one person is officially subordinate to another, the superior if he is a gentleman never thinks of it, and the subordinate if he is a gentleman never forgets it.
>
> —GEN John J. Pershing

Let's bring you into that Room of the Ages and let you ask three leadership questions to that assembled group of luminaries. It might go like this . . .

Question #1 from the young seagoing officer: "Well, room full of wise historic people, what do you believe is the MOST IMPORTANT LEADERSHIP ATTRIBUTE?"[1]

GEN ALEXANDER PATCH: The foundation of leadership is *character*.

GEN H. NORMAN SCHWARZKOPF: Leadership is a potent combination of strategy and *character*. But if you must be without one, be without the strategy.

GEN PATTON: *Moral courage* is the most valuable and usually the most absent characteristic in men.

WINSTON CHURCHILL: *Courage* is rightly esteemed the first of human qualities . . . because it is the quality that guarantees all others.

SAM WALTON: *High expectations* are the key to everything.

NAPOLEON: Be *clear*, be clear, be clear.

TONY BLAIR: The art of leadership is *saying "no,"* not "yes." It is very easy to say "yes."

EUGENE B. HABECKER, AUTHOR: The true leader *serves*. Serves people. Serves their best interests, and in so doing will not

---

[1] The answers to the young officers' questions are in the speakers' own words.

always be popular, may not always impress. But because true leaders are motivated by loving concern rather than a desire for personal glory, they are willing to pay the price.

STEPHEN GREGG, CHAIRMAN AND CEO, ETHIX CORPORATION: People do not follow uncommitted leaders. *Commitment* can be displayed in a full range of matters to include the work hours you choose to maintain, how you work to improve your abilities, or what you do for your fellow workers at personal sacrifice.

CONRAD HILTON: Success seems to be connected with *action*. Successful people keep moving. They make mistakes, but they don't quit.

THEODORE ROOSEVELT: The most important single ingredient in the formula of success is *knowing how to get along with people*.

SUN TZU: By command I mean the general's qualities of *wisdom, sincerity, humanity, courage*, and *strictness*.

DENIS WAITLEY, AUTHOR: The winner's edge is not in a gifted birth, a high IQ, or in talent. The winner's edge is all in the *attitude*, not aptitude. Attitude is the criterion for success.

HENRY GRULAND, BUSINESSMAN: Being a leader is more than just wanting to lead. Leaders have *empathy* for others and a keen ability to find the best in people . . . not the worst . . . by truly caring for others.

LEE IACOCCA: I have found that *being honest* is the best technique I can use. Right up front, tell people what you're trying to accomplish and what you're willing to sacrifice to accomplish it.

KEN BLANCHARD: The only way to develop *responsibility* in people is to give them responsibility.

SAMUEL JOHNSON: *Self-confidence* is the first requisite to great undertakings.

VADM JAMES STOCKDALE: The test of character is not "hanging in there" when you expect a light at the end of the tunnel, but *performance of duty* and *persistence* of example when you know that no light is coming.

ALBERT EINSTEIN: *Setting an example* is not the main means of influencing another; it is the only means.

DAVID LEE: *Communication* is the currency of leadership.

WARREN BENNIS: Many leaders do not have *empathy*, but . . . those that lack empathy lack the ability to move people. Leaders who can instill an atmosphere of working together gain respect, taking charge without taking control.

GEN PATTON: I can tell a commander by the way he *speaks*. He does not have to swear as much as I do, but he has to speak so that no one will refuse to follow his order.

CARLY FIORINA, CEO, HEWLETT-PACKARD: There is no substitute for *hard work*. It will always outweigh brilliance over time.

LEE IACOCCA: If I had to sum up in one word what makes a good manager, I'd say *decisiveness*.

Question #2 from the young seagoing officer: *"Wow! Lots of different attributes, all right. What other* LEADERSHIP ADVICE *do you have for me to consider?"*

RADM GRACE HOPPER: You don't manage people; you manage things. You lead people.

GEN PATTON: You young lieutenants have to realize that your platoon is like a piece of spaghetti. You can't push it. You've got to get out in front and pull it.

ADM ARLEIGH BURKE: There must be a common purpose or there can be no success.

GEN COLIN POWELL: There are no secrets to success. It is the result of preparation, hard work, and learning from failure.

ANONYMOUS SEAGOING OFFICER: You get what you inspect, not what you expect!

ADM ARLEIGH BURKE: It is imperative for . . . an officer to know his Sailors. Get to know them—know their strengths, their weaknesses, their skills, their wisdom.

SOLON: Learn to obey before you command.

ADM MOORER: A leader can gain the support of his people by telling them specifically what should and should not be done. (This does not imply how to do it—just what it is necessary to accomplish.) People do not like receiving orders that leave them uncertain of what is required of them.

WILLIAM BUTLER YEATS: Think like a wise man but communicate in the language of the people.

SAINT PAUL: Whatsoever thou doeth, do it with all thy might.

CAPT DANIEL GLADE, USA: [You] have to be the unit's leader or commander. To do that you cannot be one of the troops. They do not need another buddy. They need a leader and expect you will step up to that. Be demanding on standards and tough-minded in the way you decide and conduct yourself. Care for your troops but be a leader.

STANDING ORDER FROM HQ TO A COAST GUARD LEADER IN THE FIELD: Do what you have to do. Act first. Call me later.

ALBERT EINSTEIN: Make everything as simple as possible, but not simpler.

ANDREW CARNEGIE: No man will make a great leader who wants to do it all himself, or to get all the credit for doing it.

MARY BROWNE: Expect people to be better than they are; it helps them to become better. But don't be disappointed when they are not; it helps them to keep trying.

MARY KAY ASH: Sandwich every bit of criticism between two layers of praise.

ADM CHESTER NIMITZ: First, determine what career you want to follow, then plan it all the way to the top. Then ask for the best and toughest job available that suits your career path.

WALTER LIPPMANN: The genius of a good leader is to leave behind him a situation which common sense, without the trace of genius, can deal with successfully.

WINSTON CHURCHILL: There is great wisdom in reserving one's decision as long as possible and until all the facts and forces that will be potent at the moment are revealed.

ADM ARLEIGH BURKE: If the equipment doesn't work in battle, it doesn't make much difference how much else the officers know, the battle is lost—and so are the people in it. So—it can be right handy to be a good engineer first—and a brilliant theorist after.

MARY WALDROP: It's important that people know what you stand for. It's equally important that they know what you won't stand for.

GEN NORMAN SCHWARZKOPF: Rule 13: When put into a position of command, take charge. Rule 14: When put into a position of command, do what is right.

DWIGHT D. EISENHOWER: You do not lead by hitting people over the head—that's assault, not leadership.

JESSE JACKSON: Leadership cannot just go along to get along. Leadership must meet the moral challenge of the day.

RICHARD THORNBURGH: Subordinates cannot be left to speculate as to the values of the organization. Top leadership must give forth clear and explicit signals, lest any confusion or uncertainty exist over what is and is not permissible conduct.

GEN PATTON: When a decision has to be made, make it. There is no totally right time for anything.

BENJAMIN DISRAELI: Nurture your mind with great thoughts. To believe in the heroic makes heroes.

GEN PATTON: Commanders must remember that the issuance of an order, or the devising of a plan, is only about 5 percent of the responsibility of command. The other 95 percent is to insure [sic], by personal observation . . . that the order is carried out.

SAINT JAMES: Be swift to hear, slow to speak, slow to wrath.

MARGARET A. WHEATLEY: Power in an organization is the capacity generated by relationships.

PETER DRUCKER: If you can't measure it, then you can't manage it.

WALTER LIPPMAN: The final test of a leader is that he leaves behind him in other men the conviction and the will to carry on.

ST. AMBROSE: The wise man, before he speaks, will consider well what he speaks, to whom he speaks, and where and when.

GEN PATTON: There is a great deal of talk about loyalty from the bottom to the top. Loyalty from the top down is even more necessary and much less prevalent.

DONALD T. REGAN: You've got to give loyalty down, if you want loyalty up.

SENECA: He who has great power should use it lightly.

MARGARET CHASE SMITH: One of the basic causes for all the trouble in the world today is that people talk too much and think too little. They act impulsively without thinking. I always try to think before I talk.

WINSTON CHURCHILL: An accepted leader has only to be sure of what it is best to do, or at least to have made up his mind about it.

B. H. LIDDEL HART: A commander should have a profound understanding of human nature, the knack of smoothing out troubles, the power of winning affection while communicating energy, and the capacity for ruthless determination where required by circumstances. He needs to generate an electrifying current and to keep a cool head in applying it.

THOMAS JEFFERSON: I am a great believer in luck, and I find the harder I work the more I have of it.

GEN JOHN LEJEUNE: The relation between officers and men should in no sense be that of superior and inferior nor that of master and servant, but rather that of teacher and scholar.

THEODORE ROOSEVELT: The best executive is one who has sense enough to pick good people to do what he wants done, and self-restraint enough to keep from meddling with them while they do it.

GEN PATTON: Never tell people how to do things. Tell them what to do and they will surprise you with their ingenuity.

WINSTON CHURCHILL: Ponder, and then act.

GOETHE: Correction does much, but encouragement does more. Encouragement after censure is as the sun after a shower.

HARRY TRUMAN: It's amazing how much you can accomplish if you do not care who gets the credit.

GEN WILLIAM T. SHERMAN: The true way to be popular with troops is not to be free and familiar with them, but to make them believe you know more than they do.

RALPH WALDO EMERSON: Trust men, and they will be true to you.

THEODORE ROOSEVELT: Nobody cares how much you know, until they know how much you care.

MARY DEE HICKS: When you're in a new job where you're stretched, your focus should be on learning, not getting an A.

JOHN BUCHAN: The task of leadership is not to put greatness into humanity, but to elicit it, for the greatness is already there.

ERNEST HEMINGWAY: When people talk, listen completely. Most people never listen.

GEN NORMAN SCHWARTZKOPF: Every substandard organization I have ever seen had low performance standards. [If] you want superior performance, then you have got to set high standards.

WELSH PROVERB: He that would be a leader must be a bridge.

VADM James Stockdale: Strange as it sounds, great leaders gain authority by giving it away.

John C. Maxwell: Competence goes beyond words. It's the leader's ability to say it, plan it, and do it in such a way that others know you know how—and know that they want to follow you.

Theodore Roosevelt: Do what you can, where you are at, with what you have.

Confucius: Respect yourself and others will respect you.

ADM Arleigh Burke: Success cannot be administered.

Lord Nelson: Recollect that you must be a seaman to be an officer; and also that you cannot be a good officer without being a gentleman.

Weeks: "An officer and a gentleman" is a familiar term to everyone both in and out of the Service. Be sure you are both. You cannot be an officer and a gentleman unless you are just, humane, thoroughly trained, unless you have character, a high sense of honor, and an unselfish devotion to duty. Be an example of such to everyone.

Xenophon: No one can be a good officer who does not undergo more than those he commands.

John C. Maxwell: A good leader encourages followers to tell him what he needs to know, not what he wants to hear.

Question #3 from the young seagoing officer: *"My head is spinning! Thanks for that leadership advice. But one last thing. I'm new—I screw up a lot. I worry about making mistakes as I learn how to be a leader. Any thoughts on MISTAKES?"*

Elbert Hubbard, author: The greatest mistake one can make in life is to be continually fearing you will make one.

Theodore Roosevelt: The only man who never makes a mistake is the man who never does anything.

Weston H. Agor: Making mistakes simply means you are learning faster.

DAVID B. PETERSON: The more you crash, the more you learn.

DR. LINUS PAULING: The best way to have a good idea is to have a lot of ideas.

THOMAS WATSON SR., FOUNDER, IBM: The fastest way to succeed is to double the failure rate.

GEN BRUCE C. CLARKE: You must be able to underwrite the honest mistakes of your subordinates if you wish to develop their initiative and experience.

ROBERT F. KENNEDY: Only those who dare to fail greatly can ever achieve greatly.

THEODORE ROOSEVELT: He who makes no mistakes, makes no progress.

CHAPTER 10

BECOMING THE LEADER
YOU WANT TO BE

The greatest problem facing the career naval officer is leadership. Yet this most important factor in an [officer's] life frequently is allowed to grow like a choice flower in a garden surrounded by rank weeks.

So many feel that if they follow the average course of naval life, experience will finally give them the qualities of a great leader. . . . Few realize that the growth to sound leadership is a life's work.

Ambition alone will not encompass it. . . . The path to qualification for leadership [at sea] is a long, hard road to travel. It is a path of life.

—ADM WILLIAM V. PRATT

L et's return to the two points made in previous chapters.
First, you can become the leader you want to be.
Second, it's not rocket science. You can acquire leadership skills, if you choose to. Remember SPOM: Study, Practice, Observation, Mentorship.

You are now, officially, as you read these words, at a junction point in your life. You can go two ways.

You can be one of the 90 percent of junior officers who will read these words, put this book down, and probably never think about it again.

Or you can be one of the 10 percent who resolve to create a plan to be all the leader that he or she can be.

> You've got to be careful if you don't know where you're going, because you might not get there.
>
> —*Yogi Berra*

If you're one of the 90 percent I hope this book was helpful in some way, and I hope you'll put it on your bookshelf for future reference. Good luck in the fleet!

If you're one of the 10 percent or are considering being in that select group, read on for these last few pages . . .

HOW TO BECOME THE LEADER YOU WANT TO BE

Hopefully by now you're convinced that leadership is important. Important to your ship, your career, and your path of service. If you want to be a better leader, then there are three simple steps to take.

Step One: Decide What Leadership Means to You

Decide on your own description of the leader you want to be. What is *your* definition? *Your* list of traits and attributes and skills and practices? Don't make it too lengthy—I recommend against the "one hundred attributes of a leader" school. Instead, think of ten or a dozen things that are important to you, perhaps in categories, or buckets.

Here's one example of a leadership model:

ENS Kathy Sullivan on a Navy destroyer believes that leadership is about two buckets: *traits* and *skills*. She has drawn up her list of her five most important *traits* and seven most valued *skills* in the matrix on the next page.

This is Kathy's own personal leadership model. A model doesn't have to be fancy. But it does have to be personal. What works for others won't necessarily work for her.

Traits	Skills
Honesty	Communication
Compassion	Delegation
Work Ethic	Listening
Loyalty	Team Building
Sense of Humor	Inciting Fun
	Planning
	Caring for People

Here's another example:

LT (jg) Mike Herbert is on a Coast Guard cutter. He's most comfortable with the Be-Know-Do model of leadership. The buckets on his personal leadership list are threefold: who you are (Be), your skill sets (Know), and your actions (Do). For him, each bucket has four items to remember. He likes the model because he can recite it using the fingers of one hand, and the three buckets, with four items each, equal a perfect dozen.

BE (Who you are)	KNOW (Your skill sets)	DO (Your actions)
Courageous	Great ship-driver	Set goals
Team player	Excellent navigator	Drive hard
Honest	Delegation	Care for the troops
Loyal	Communication	Get the job done

Mike's model is different from Kathy's, but it doesn't matter, because it works for him.

The important thing is to have your own model. It doesn't have to last a lifetime—it'll change, I promise. But if you want to be a leader, you need to decide for yourself what being a leader is.

In the space below, take ten minutes and write down what your personal leadership model might look like. Pick from one to four buckets. Pick from one to seven items per bucket. Fill it in. Try it out!

Bucket				
1				
2				
3				
4				
5				
6				
7				

Now that you've built your own leadership model, let's move to the next step.

Step Two: Determine Where You Need Improvement

Once you have a rough picture of what you think a leader should be, it's time to assess yourself to find where you need improvement. To use business-speak jargon, it's time for a "gap analysis" between the "as is" (what you are today) and the "to be" (what you want to be). How can you determine where you need improvement?

The first method is self-assessment. You'll probably have some innate sense of what you're good at and where you're weak. Do an honest, gut-feel assessment of where you stand vis-à-vis each of your desired traits and skills. Are you honest? Do you really care about your folks? Are you good at delegating, or are you a micromanager? Are you willing to give recognition to others, even when it means people don't know how well you did personally?

The second method is through mentoring and advice from friends. Find a confidant peer or a senior whom you trust, and ask him or her: "How am I at delegating? How strong or weak am I at X, Y, and Z? If I had to improve in three areas, what would they be?" Most people will push back and will be reluctant to offer you constructive criticism, for fear they'll lose you as a friend. Get past this. The best thing they can do is give you the feedback you need. I've found that when I ask people (seniors or peers) to give me three palpable suggestions for improvement, they'll eventually cough them up, if I am adamant about it.

By the way, when they do finally offer some suggestions, don't be defensive! Don't attack them! Just be grateful, and thank them.

The third method of self-analysis is through proactive 360-degree feedback. In this case you ask your peers, your seniors, and your subordinates to grade you on your leadership traits and skills. You can make up a survey, or you can go on the web to purchase a service to provide it. These surveys are confidential, and if properly administered, they're the best way to get unfiltered feedback. They're the most work to make happen, but they will provide the best information for your game plan.

> Anyone who stops learning is old, whether at twenty or eighty. Anyone who keeps learning stays young. The greatest thing in life is to keep your mind young.
>
> —*Henry Ford*

Let's say you've identified ten leadership skills you feel are part of the leader you want to be. Your goal is to decide where you're average, where you're strong, and where you're weak. Those three levels of skills are sufficient. Your initial game plan will be to work on your weak areas.

Step Three: Fix It through a Long-Term SPOM Game Plan

Once you've identified where you need some improvement, it's time to build a brief SPOM game plan. Remember, SPOM is Study, Practice, Observation, and Mentorship. The plan doesn't have to be voluminous or overwhelming. Let's say you've decided that one of your weaknesses as a leader is your difficulty in establishing personal connections with your people.

Your plan to work on that could be as simple as the following:

Study. Read a book on personal connections, such as *Emotional Intelligence* by Daniel Goleman or *How to Win Friends and Influence People* by Dale Carnegie. Theodore Roosevelt, who was a voracious reader, said, "I am a part of everything I have read." Conversely everything you read becomes a part of you! Your reading is a diet for your brain; pick the right things.

Practice. Once a month, invite one of the members in the division to lunch and talk about his or her issues and concerns and needs and plans. Practice using the techniques and tips you read about.

Observation. Watch and learn from the chief engineer, who seems to be a whiz at connecting with people and understanding where they are and what they need. How does she do that?

Mentorship. Stop by the captain's cabin twice a year and ask for advice on how to be better at making connections. Ask for feedback from his perspective.

That's it. Again, doesn't have to be complicated. No calculus involved. Doesn't take a PhD. It simply means identifying some weakness, some area in which you want to improve, and taking the moments of time it takes to get better in that area.

If you were a high school basketball player and were great at running and dribbling and shooting from inside, but couldn't hit a free throw to save your life, what would you do? You'd study free throws. You'd practice shooting free throws. You'd observe others who were good free-throw shooters. And you'd get your coaches to show you how to shoot free throws. And, as a result, you'd become a better free-throw shooter and a better player overall.

So it is with your leadership skills. Only, in the vast scheme of things, shipboard leadership skills are so very, very much more important than high school basketball skills. They deserve that much more attention.

Be Like Ben Franklin

Remember Ben Franklin? Writer, printer, businessman, inventor, statesman, diplomat. A Renaissance man among Renaissance men—one of the most talented and gifted Americans ever. Ben wasn't necessarily born as talented as he was later—he became that way. Do you know that Ben had his own version of the three-step improvement method described above?

In his *Autobiography* Ben writes about how he was intent on bettering himself. He admitted being committed to "the bold and arduous project of arriving at Moral Perfection." He created his own list of thirteen virtues: Temperance, Silence, Order, Resolution, Frugality, Industry, Sincerity, Justice, Moderation, Cleanliness, Tranquility, Chastity, and Humility. Each week he concentrated on a single virtue, so that in the course of fifty-two weeks, he'd go through the list four times. He kept a notebook and each week would write down his successes and failures. He studied the virtues, he practiced them, he observed them in others, he sought advice from others. He identified where he wanted to be stronger, and he employed a SPOM methodology to become better.

It was good enough for Ben. It should be good enough for you, too!

A Sample One-Page Plan

Let's look at a simple example of a junior officer improvement program. Say ENS Kathy Sullivan, in the previous example, has listed her desired traits and skills and has done some analysis and soul-searching to see how she stacks up against her model of a young leader. Here are her preliminary results:

	Attribute	Comparison to Goal	Action Plan
TRAITS	Honesty	Great! Above average	
	Compassion	Average	
	Work Ethic	Slightly weak	Need work, probably
	Loyalty	Above average—strong	
	Sense of Humor	Below average!	Need work
SKILL SETS	Communication	Slightly below average	Need work
	Delegation	Terrible. I stink here!	Need lots of work!
	Listening	Good at this . . .	
	Team Building	Good here	
	Inciting Fun	Great! Above average	
	Planning	Below average	Need work
	Caring for People	Good here	

As you can see, it doesn't have to be lengthy or complicated. Just decide where you want to be better. In this case, Kathy has decided that of her twelve leadership traits and skills, she needs work on five of them.

The greatest discovery of my generation is that human beings can alter their lives by altering their attitude of mind.

—*William James, psychologist*

Once you've identified where you need work, then decide what to do. How can one improve?

Read a book. Listen to a CD. Scan the web. Talk to a mentor. Take a class. Ask a friend for advice. Ask your boss for advice. Use your head—think! Whatever you do, come up with your own action plan.

Here's Kathy's example:

	Attribute	Comparison to Goal	Action Plan
TRAITS	Honesty	Great! Above average	
	Compassion	Average	
	Work Ethic	Slightly weak	Talk to the skipper; start work 30 min. earlier each day
	Loyalty	Above average—strong	
	Sense of Humor	Below average!	Go to jokes.com; memorize ten jokes; practice one/week!
SKILL SETS	Communication	Slightly below average	Read the book *Give Your Speech, Change the World*
	Delegation	Terrible. I stink here!	Listen to the "One Minute Manager" on CD
	Listening	Good at this . . .	
	Team Building	Good here	
	Inciting Fun	Great! Above average	
	Planning	Below average	Go to the one-day planning course the CHENG told me about . . .
	Caring for People	Good here	

When you're done with those areas, think of other actions that can make you better. As you progress as a leader, you'll find other weaknesses you'll want to work on. The exercise above is not a one-time event—it's something you do again and again. It's a habit that will get you where you want to go.

Now, dear seagoing officer readers: you're sophisticated, you're smart, you're savvy. The above exercise perhaps seems too silly, too simple to be useful. "Write down what I want to improve in?" you ask. Seems hardly worth the time.

That's where you're wrong. Statistical studies show that someone who writes something down, however simply, is more likely to get it done. If a person determines in his head that he wants to lose fifteen pounds, his chances of actually losing it go up dramatically if he writes it down and posts that note where he can see it daily. Sounds unbelievable, but it's fact. There is power in the declaration in writing, even if the writing is only a note to yourself.

A Proposed Leadership Model for You, the Young Officer at Sea

We've reviewed multiple models, and I've asked you to pick one, or invent one. Before you do, here's a potential model just for you. It's based on the cumulative results of this book. For ease of memory, think of a star, or think of the memory aid STEAM.

For you, the young officer, your leadership model could be broken into the five points of a star, the first initials of which spell the word "steam." (By the way, it also spells "teams," if that's easier to remember!)

Courage is contagious. When a brave man takes a stand, the spines of others are stiffened.

—*Billy Graham*

The five pillars of this potential leadership model:

S: Skills on the Job
- professional competence
- knowledge

T: Team competencies
- project management
- team building skills
- ability to get along with others
- followership

E: Ethics and Character
- honesty and integrity
- dependability
- trustworthiness

A: Attitude
- work ethic
- optimism
- discipline
- initiative
- perseverance

M: Management competencies
- delegation
- receiving (listening)
- transmitting (spoken and written)

This is just one more model for you to consider. If you want to use this model, and choose to implement a SPOM action plan, a sample action plan is provided in appendix A.

Regardless of what model you choose—regardless of what kind of action plan you write—take an hour of your busy life and make a plan for the rest of your life. As the Chinese proverb goes, "the journey of a thousand miles begins with a single step." Or, as some of my seagoing friends have (correctly) noted, "A failure to plan is a plan to fail." You've already set yourself apart by reading this far in the book. So continue that with the last and final step—your own personal action plan for growing as a leader.

Unfortunately most of you won't do it. But if you want to be in that top 10 percent or in that top 1 percent you *must* do things that most people don't do. Planning, studying, taking prepared action are part of it. A half hour a week to improve your leadership skills will, over a couple years, set you apart.

———————⚓———————

Theodore Roosevelt was a sickly child. Through will and tenacity he made himself into the "rough rider" and outdoorsman. He eventually led troops in the Spanish-American War, he led our Navy as assistant secretary of the Navy, and ultimately he led our country. He said, "With self-discipline, most anything is possible."

He overcame much with self-discipline. Self-discipline can make you the leader you want to be. All you have to do is overcome the inertia of the next hour.

If you want it, you can do it.

It follows then, as certain as night succeeds day, that without a decisive naval force we can do nothing definitive, and with it everything honorable and glorious.

—GEN George Washington

CLOSING

So there you go. We looked briefly at the six basic questions on leadership.

We reviewed ten thousand pages of books, which cumulatively demonstrated common themes of what it means to be a leader—common attributes, common skill sets, common actions and habits.

We polled 380 senior seagoing leaders on what they think is most important in a young seagoing officer like you. They valued integrity and character above all else. But when their six thousand votes and nine thousand years of experience were boiled down to their essence, what they really wanted in a young new officer on their ship was: An Honest, Hard-Working Teammate.

We reviewed dozens of sea stories and bits of leadership advice from those same stories because, as you'll remind yourself, parables are a great way to learn lessons. And, in the school of hard knocks, if you can learn from someone else's knocks, so much the better!

We listened to leadership advice provided over the last two thousand years from presidents, industrialists, statesmen, admirals, and generals.

And, finally, we looked in this chapter at how a young seagoing officer like you might begin to follow in the footsteps of other great leaders who started out just like you: new, learning, trying to understand the art, and the science, of leadership and of getting others to do what you want them to do—the things in life that need to be done, but won't get done, without the catalyst of leadership.

I hope that you take to heart the three truths discussed in the first chapter:

Leadership is important.

Leadership can be defined and described.

Leadership can be learned.

Leadership is, indeed, important. Arguably it is the most salient and necessary part of your seagoing career. It is definable, even though definitions vary according to the leader and the circumstance. And, most vital to you, it can be learned.

You *can* be the leader you want to be—the leader your ship needs you to be—the leader your people and your shipmates need you to be; perhaps even the leader your country needs you to be.

Perhaps this book has helped you cast off the lines as you depart on your voyage toward being a leader. I hope your course proves straight and true and that you reach your intended destination. Fair winds and following seas!

A SPOM ACTION PLAN
FOR THE STEAM LEADERSHIP MODEL

Leadership Area	My Assessment	My Intended Improvements
S: Skills on the Job		
Professional Knowledge		
Everyday Job Skills		
Other:		
T: Team competencies		
Project Management		
Team Building		
Getting Along with Others		
Other:		
E: Ethics and Character		
Honesty and Integrity		
Trustworthiness		
Other:		

Leadership Area	My Assessment	My Intended Improvements
A: Attitude		
Work Ethic		
Optimism		
Discipline		
Initiative		
Perseverance		
Other:		
M: Management competencies		
Delegation		
Listening		
Speaking		
Writing		
Planning/Goal Setting		
Other:		

THE THIRTY-FIVE LEADERSHIP BOOKS

The Sea Service Books

The Blue Jacket's Manual
By Thomas J. Cutler
Naval Institute Press, Annapolis, MD, 2002.
648 pages.

Character in Action: The Coast Guard on Leadership
By Donald T. Phillips and ADM James M. Loy,
USCG (Ret.)
Naval Institute Press, Annapolis, MD, 2003.
178 pages.

Coast Guard Leadership Development Framework
Commandant Instruction M5351.3 of May 2006.

Command at Sea (6th edition)
By ADM James Stavridis, USN, and RDML Robert
Girrier, USN (Ret.)
Naval Institute Press, Annapolis, MD, 2010.
400 pages.

*Division Officers Guide: A Handbook for Junior Officers and
Petty Officers in the U.S. Navy and the U.S. Coast Guard
(11th edition)*
By VADM James Stavridis, USN, and CDR Robert
Girrier, USN
Naval Institute Press, Annapolis, MD, 2004. 352 pages.

Fundamentals of Naval Leadership
By the Department of Leadership and Law, U.S. Naval
Academy
Edited by Professor Karel Montor and MAJ Anthony
J. Ciotti, USMC
Naval Institute Press, Annapolis, MD, 1984. 276 pages.

*Leadership Embodied: The Secrets to Success of the Most
Effective Navy and Marine Corps Leaders*
> Edited by LTC Joseph J. Thomas
> Naval Institute Press, Annapolis, MD, 2005. 211 pages.

Naval Leadership: Voices of Experience
> Edited by Karel Montor, CAPT Thomas McNicholas,
> USN, LTC Anthony Ciotti, USMC, LCDR Thomas
> Hutchinson, USNR, and Jackie Eckhart Wehmueller
> Naval Institute Press, Annapolis, MD, 1987.
> 500 pages.

The Naval Officer's Guide (12th edition)
> By CDR Lesa A. McComas, USN (Ret.)
> Naval Institute Press, Annapolis, MD, 2011.
> 394 pages.

Navy Leader Planning Guide
> Center for Personal and Professional Development,
> Norfolk, VA, 2010.

Leadership Books from Other Services

The Armed Forces Officer
> U.S. Department of Defense
> National Defense University Press and Potomac Books,
> Washington, DC, 2007. 162 pages.

*Coast Guard Commandant Instruction M5351.3: Leadership
Development Framework.*
> May 2006.

*Ethics and the Military Profession: Moral Foundations of
Leadership*
> (Air Force Academy edition)
> Edited by Dr. George R. Lucas Jr. and CAPT W. Rick
> Rubel, USN (Ret.)
> Pearson/Longman, Boston, MA, 2006. 554 pages.

Field Manual 1-0, Leading Marines
FMFM 1–0, DON, HQ USMC, 1995.

Muddy Boots Leadership: Real-Life Stories and Personal Examples of Good, Bad, and Unexpected Results
By MAJ John Chapman, USA
Stackpole Books, Mechanicsburg, PA, 2006. 174 pages.

The U.S. Army Leadership Field Manual
U.S. Army FM 22–100
McGraw Hill, New York, 2004. 212 pages.

Leadership Books from Business and Academia

The AMA Handbook of Leadership
By Marshall Goldsmith, John Baldoni, and Sarah McArthur
American Management Association, New York, 2010. 288 pages.

Churchill on Leadership
By Steven F. Hayward
Prima Publishing, Rocklin, CA, 1998. 202 pages.

The Contrarian's Guide to Leadership
By Stephen B. Sample
Jossey-Bass, San Francisco, CA, 2002. 224 pages.

The Effective Executive: The Definitive Guide to Getting the Right Things Done
By Peter F. Drucker
HarperCollins, New York, [1967] 2006. 178 pages.

It's Your Ship
By CAPT D. Michael Abrashoff
Warner Books, New York, 2002. 212 pages.

Leadership: Enhancing the Lessons of Experience
By Richard L. Hughes, Robert C. Ginnett, and Gordon J. Curphy
McGraw-Hill Irwin, Boston, MA, 2006. 592 pages.

*The Leadership Challenge: How to Keep Getting
Extraordinary Things Done in Organizations*
By James M. Kouzes and Barry Z. Posner
Jossey-Bass Publishers, San Francisco, CA, 1995.
432 pages.

Leadership for Dummies
By Marshall Loeb and Stephen Kindel
Wylie Publishing, Hoboken, NJ, 1999. 358 pages.

*The Leadership Lessons of Jesus: A Timeless Model for Today's
Leaders*
By Bob Briner and Ray Pritchard
Broadman & Holman, Nashville, TN, 1997. 240 pages.

Leadership Lessons of the White House Fellows
By Charles P. Garcia
McGraw-Hill, New York, 2009. 288 pages.

*Leadership Mastery: How to Challenge Yourself and Others to
Greatness*
Dale Carnegie Training
Simon & Schuster, New York, 2000. 256 pages.

The Nature of Leadership
Edited by John Antonakis, Anna T. Cianciolo, and
Robert J. Sternberg
SAGE Publications, Thousand Oaks, CA, 2004.
438 pages.

Patton on Leadership
By Alan Axelrod
Prentice Hall Press, Paramus, NJ, 1999. 304 pages.

*Preparing to Lead: Principles of Self-Leadership and
Organizational Dynamics*
Contributing editors: COL Arthur Athens, Dr. Donnie
Horner, LT Brett St. George, CDR Steve Trainor,
LT Joy Watkins, and LT Kerri Chase
Pearson Education, Boston, 2006.

The Rules of Management: A Definitive Code for Managerial Success
>   By Richard Templar
>   Pearson Prentice Hall, NJ, 2005. 208 pages.

Semper Fi: Business Leadership the Marine Corps Way
>   By Dan Carrison and Rod Walsh
>   American Management Association, New York, 1999.
>   240 pages.

Successful Executive's Handbook
>   By Susan H. Gebelein, David G. Lee, Kristie J. Nelson-
>   Heuhaus, and Elaine B. Sloan
>   Personnel Decisions International Corporation,
>   Minneapolis, MN, 1999. 473 pages.

The Transformational Leader
>   By Noel M. Tichy and Mary Anne DeVanna
>   John Wiley & Sons, New York, 1990. 306 pages.

The 21 Indispensable Qualities of a Leader: Becoming the Person Others Will Want to Follow
>   By John C. Maxwell
>   Thomas Nelson Publishers, Nashville, TN, 1999.
>   176 pages.

A GREAT LEADERSHIP LIST: TRAITS AND ATTRIBUTES

In his book *Leadership Embodied: The Secrets to Success of the Most Effective Navy and Marine Corps Leaders,* LTC Joseph Thomas, USMC, provides stories about great Navy and Marine Corp leaders who embodied certain traits or attributes that we associate with leadership. It's a long list, but a good one, and is provided here.

Traits and Stories of Those Who Embodied Them

1. Initiative: Lambert Wickes
2. Tenacity: John Paul Jones
3. Boldness and Resourcefulness: Stephen Decatur
4. Perseverance and Resourcefulness: Joshua Barney
5. Perseverance in Adversity: Oliver Hazard Perry
6. Dynamic Intellect: Matthew Fontaine Maury
7. Military Bearing: Matthew Calbraith Perry
8. Inspiration: David Glasgow Farragut
9. Daring: William B. Cushing
10. Scholarship: Stephen B. Luce
11. Commitment: Theodorus Bailey Myers Mason
12. Foresight: George Dewey
13. Knowledge: Theodore Roosevelt
14. Professionalism: Alfred Thayer Mahan
15. Pedagogy: John A. Lejeune
16. Insight: Earl H. Ellis
17. Vision: William A. Moffett
18. Drive: Lewis B. Puller
19. Adaptation: William F. Halsey
20. Teamwork: Slade D. Cutter

21. Dedication: Joseph J. Rochefort
22. Intuition: Clarence W. McClusky
23. Focus: Joseph J. Foss
24. Moral Courage: Archer A. Vandegrift
25. Intellectual Analysis: Mary Sears
26. Presence: Lewis W. Walt
27. Skilled Warfighting: Marc A. Mitscher
28. Tactical Proficiency: Willis A. Lee Jr.
29. Ambition: Ernest J. King
30. Accountability: Charles B. McVay III
31. Loyalty: Chester W. Nimitz
32. Analytical Thinking: Raymond A. Spruance
33. Vision: Victor H. Krulak
34. Pioneering Spirit: Joy Bright Hancock
35. Personal Growth: Hyman G. Rickover
36. Moral Courage: Merritt A. Edson
37. Innovative Problem Solving: Charles B. Momsen
38. Instinct: Arleigh A. Burke
39. Endurance: Raymond G. Davis
40. Responsiveness: James H. Doyle
41. Technical Innovator: Grace Murray Hopper
42. Perseverance in the Face of Discrimination:
    Carl M. Brashear
43. Conviction: Thomas H. Moorer
44. Courage: Ulysses S. Grant Sharp
45. Setting the Precedent: Samuel L. Gravely Jr.
46. Physical Courage: Ronald McKeown
47. Innovation: Elmo R. Zumwalt Jr.
48. Passion: John F. Lehman Jr.
49. Integrity: Leighton W. Smith

ANOTHER GREAT LEADERSHIP LIST:
ADVICE AND RULES

In the book *The Rules of Management: A Definitive Code for Managerial Success,* author Richard Templar creates a "code" of one hundred practices and rules for excellence in management. His view of management includes many attributes considered as leadership. He breaks his list into two buckets: manage your team and manage yourself.

Manage Your Team
1. Get them emotionally involved.
2. Know what a team is and how it works.
3. Set realistic targets—no, really realistic.
4. Hold effective meetings—no, really effective.
5. Make meetings fun.
6. Make your team better than you.
7. Set your boundaries.
8. Be ready to cut.
9. Offload as much as you can—or dare.
10. Let them make mistakes.
11. Accept their limitations.
12. Encourage people.
13. Be very, very good at finding the right people.
14. Take the rap.
15. Give credit to the team when it deserves it.
16. Get the best resources for your team.
17. Celebrate.
18. Keep track of everything you do and say.
19. Be sensitive to friction.
20. Create a good atmosphere.

21. Inspire loyalty and team spirit.
22. Fight for your team.
23. Have and show trust in your staff.
24. Respect individual differences.
25. Listen to ideas from others.
26. Adapt your style to each team member.
27. Let them think they know more than you (even if they don't).
28. Don't always expect to have the last word.
29. Understand the roles of others.
30. Ensure people know exactly what is expected of them.
31. Use positive reinforcement to motivate.
32. Don't try justifying stupid systems.
33. Be ready to say yes.
34. Train them to bring you solutions, not problems.

Manage Yourself

35. Get it done, work hard.
36. Set an example and standards.
37. Enjoy yourself.
38. Don't let it get to you.
39. Know what you are supposed to be doing.
40. Know what you are actually doing.
41. Be proactive, not reactive.
42. Be consistent.
43. Set realistic targets for yourself—no, really realistic.
44. Have a game plan, but keep it secret.
45. Get rid of superfluous rules.
46. Learn from your mistakes.
47. Be ready to unlearn—what works, changes.
48. Cut the crap—prioritize.
49. Cultivate those in the know.
50. Know when to shut the door.

51. Fill your time productively and profitably.

52. Have a plan B and a plan C.

53. Capitalize on chance—be lucky, but never admit it.

54. Recognize when you're stressed.

55. Manage your health.

56. Be prepared for the pain and the pleasure.

57 Face the future.

58. Head up, not head down.

59. See the wood and the trees.

60. Know when to let go.

61. Be decisive, even if it means being wrong sometimes.

62. Adopt minimalism as a management style.

63. Visualize your blue plaque.

64. Have principles and stick to them.

65. Follow your intuition, your gut instinct.

66. Be creative.

67. Don't stagnate.

68. Be flexible and ready to move on.

69. Remember the object of the exercise.

70. Remember that none of us has to be here.

71. Go home.

72. Keep learning—especially from the opposition.

73. Be passionate and bold.

74. Plan for the worst, but hope for the best.

75. Let the company see you are on its side.

76. Don't bad-mouth your boss.

77. Don't bad-mouth your team.

78. Accept that some things bosses tell you to do will be wrong.

79. Accept that bosses are as scared as you are at times.

80. Avoid straitjacket thinking.

81. Act and talk as if you are one of them.

82. Show you understand the viewpoint of underlings and overlings.

83. Don't back down—be prepared to stand your ground.
84. Don't play politics.
85. Don't put down other managers.
86. Share what you know.
87. Don't intimidate.
88. Be above interdepartmental warfare.
89. Show that you'll fight to the death for your team.
90. Aim for respect rather than being liked.
91. Do one or two things well and avoid the rest.
92. Seek feedback on your performance.
93. Maintain good relationships and friendships.
94. Build respect—both ways—between you and your customers.
95. Go the extra mile for your customers.
96. Be aware of your responsibilities and stick to your principles.
97. Be straight at all times and speak the truth.
98. Don't cut corners—you'll get caught.
99. Be in command and take charge.
100. Be a diplomat for the company.

INDEX

About the Author

Robert Wray, a Naval Academy graduate, served as a nuclear engineer on surface ships. He transitioned to the Reserves and enjoyed a varied civilian career in manufacturing, services, hospitality, politics, and consulting. He simultaneously progressed in his Reserve career until promoted to admiral and placed back onto full-time duty. He holds a master's degree in leadership from Georgetown and speaks and writes on the subject.

The Naval Institute Press is the book-publishing arm of the U.S. Naval Institute, a private, nonprofit, membership society for sea service professionals and others who share an interest in naval and maritime affairs. Established in 1873 at the U.S. Naval Academy in Annapolis, Maryland, where its offices remain today, the Naval Institute has members worldwide.

Members of the Naval Institute support the education programs of the society and receive the influential monthly magazine *Proceedings* or the colorful bimonthly magazine *Naval History* and discounts on fine nautical prints and on ship and aircraft photos. They also have access to the transcripts of the Institute's Oral History Program and get discounted admission to any of the Institute-sponsored seminars offered around the country.

The Naval Institute's book-publishing program, begun in 1898 with basic guides to naval practices, has broadened its scope to include books of more general interest. Now the Naval Institute Press publishes about seventy titles each year, ranging from how-to books on boating and navigation to battle histories, biographies, ship and aircraft guides, and novels. Institute members receive significant discounts on the Press's more than eight hundred books in print.

Full-time students are eligible for special half-price membership rates. Life memberships are also available.

For a free catalog describing Naval Institute Press books currently available, and for further information about joining the U.S. Naval Institute, please write to:

Member Services
U.S. Naval Institute
291 Wood Road
Annapolis, MD 21402-5034
Telephone: (800) 233-8764
Fax: (410) 571-1703
Web address: www.usni.org